Exploring Game Mechanics

Principles and Techniques to Make Fun, Engaging Games

Maithili Dhule

Apress®

Exploring Game Mechanics: Principles and Techniques to Make Fun, Engaging Games

Maithili Dhule
Singapore, Singapur, Singapore

ISBN-13 (pbk): 978-1-4842-8872-6   ISBN-13 (electronic): 978-1-4842-8873-3
https://doi.org/10.1007/978-1-4842-8873-3

Managing Director, Apress Media LLC: Welmoed Spahr
Acquisitions Editor: Spandana Chatterjee
Development Editor: Spandana Chatterjee
Coordinating Editor: Mark Powers

Cover designed by eStudioCalamar

Cover image by Josh Durham on Unsplash (www.urᴊsplash.com)

Distributed to the book trade worldwide by Apress Media, LLC, 1 New York Plaza, New York, NY 10004, U.S.A. Phone 1-800-SPRINGER, fax (201) 348-4505, e-mail orders-ny@springer-sbm.com, or visit www.springeronline.com. Apress Media, LLC is a California LLC and the sole member (owner) is Springer Science + Business Media Finance Inc (SSBM Finance Inc). SSBM Finance Inc is a **Delaware** corporation.

For information on translations, please e-mail booktranslations@springernature.com; for reprint, paperback, or audio rights, please e-mail bookpermissions@springernature.com.

Apress titles may be purchased in bulk for academic, corporate, or promotional use. eBook versions and licenses are also available for most titles. For more information, reference our Print and eBook Bulk Sales web page at http://www.apress.com/bulk-sales.

Any source code or other supplementary material referenced by the author in this book is available to readers on GitHub (https://github.com/Apress). For more detailed information, please visit http://www.apress.com/source-code.

Printed on acid-free paper

Dedicated to my family, friends, and gamers everywhere!

Table of Contents

About the Author

Maithili Dhule is an engineer by profession, writer by choice, and an aspiring game developer at heart. She is the author of *Beginning Game Development with Godot*, a beginner's guide to creating and publishing a 2D Platform game from scratch. After a friend introduced her to the art of creating games, it quickly found itself on her list of passions. In her free time, she can be found creating a new game, designing pixel art or being immersed in one of her favorite gaming titles. She also enjoys trying out new restaurants, sketching portraits, writing poetry, and going for runs while listening to a good music playlist. A browser-based game that she has developed called "Dragon's Flight" is playable on the website https://itch.io. You can reach out to her at mathletmakesgames@gmail.com.

About the Technical Reviewer

Simon Jackson is a long-time software engineer and architect with many years of Unity game development experience, as well as an author of several Unity game development titles. He loves to both create Unity projects as well as lend a hand to help educate others, whether it's via a blog, vlog, user group, or major speaking event.

His primary focus at the moment is with the XRTK (Mixed Reality Toolkit) project, which is aimed at building a cross-platform Mixed Reality framework to enable both VR and AR developers to build efficient solutions in Unity and then build/distribute them to as many platforms as possible.

Acknowledgments

If I have seen further than others, it is by standing on the shoulders of giants.

—Sir Isaac Newton

Who we are and what we do is greatly influenced by the important people in our lives. Every person we come across changes us in many subtle ways, pushing us to be better and inspiring us to be the best version of ourselves.

I'm immensely grateful toward a lot of people for making this book come to fruition.

I would like to thank my family for being supportive and patient, and for motivating me while I spent back-breaking hours working on the manuscript!

I am grateful to my friends (all around the world!) for making me laugh and smile, and for always believing in me.

I feel lucky to have been taught by so many wonderful teachers over the years. Thank you for teaching me, inspiring me, and making me capable enough to write a book!

Shortly after publishing my first book, *Beginning Game Development with Godot*, I got a chance to work on another one. I am immensely grateful to my acquisition editor, Spandana Chatterjee, for giving me this opportunity to combine my passion for writing and gaming. I would also like to thank my technical reviewer, Simon Jackson, for taking the effort to go through the entire book and suggesting valuable feedback. Moreover, I am thankful to Mark Powers, Sowmya Thodur, and the rest of the Apress team for their collaboration and help.

ACKNOWLEDGMENTS

Finally, I would like to thank Luis Zuno (Ansimuz), Paul Laulhe (Quaternius), Prakasit Khuansuwan (jcomp/Johnstocker), and the image designers on Freepik for letting me use their beautiful game assets in the book.

Thank you all for making my dream a reality!

Introduction

Gaming is an ever-expanding billion-dollar industry. Its success can be credited to the fact that everyone – young, old, somewhere in between – loves playing games! If you like games with colorful, pixel graphics and upbeat, Chiptune music, you have nostalgia-filled classics like Super Mario Bros., Pac-Man, and Space Invaders that you can play. If you're into casual mobile gaming, you have great titles like Candy Crush, Clash of Clans, Among Us, and Angry Birds. On the other hand, if you prefer something with realistic graphics, immersive storylines, and memorable characters, there are tons of AAA gaming franchises that can suit your liking such as Uncharted, The Elder Scrolls, Fallout, and Halo.

Every game is unique and has the potential to provide an amazing feeling of achievement. To understand what makes games so appealing to gamers, we can break them down into their fundamental nuts and bolts – their mechanics. No matter how complex the game, it leverages on the basic need of any gamer – to successfully complete a task that's clear and easy to understand. By focusing on how gamers think and by looking into the mechanics of popular games, we can get a better idea of how to create content that is more engaging and enjoyable.

Only when you dive deep into the design of how something works do you truly appreciate the work of its creator. Come and join me on this journey, readers, gamers, and developers, as we take a closer look at the world of game design.

I hope you enjoy reading this book as much as I enjoyed writing it!

CHAPTER 1

Why Do We Play Games?

In this chapter, we'll talk about how games satisfy some of the most essential needs of the player. We'll discuss how different kinds of game mechanics can help make gameplay interesting and exciting, and take a look at how famous games implement them. We'll also try to understand the appeal behind various gaming genres such as Casual and Puzzle, Strategy and Simulation, Action-Adventure, and Role-Playing Games.

It's All About the Player's Needs

Why do billions of people spend hours every day clicking buttons to move pixels on a screen? As gamers, what drives us to *grind* in-game to repeatedly do seemingly mundane chores such as cooking food, cleaning, chopping wood, gathering resources, farming, and traveling long distances? How do such tasks, some of which we rarely do in real life, become strangely enjoyable in the game? To answer these questions, we need to understand the psychology behind player motivation. By playing games, players hope to satisfy some of their essential emotional needs, such as

© Maithili Dhule 2022
M. Dhule, *Exploring Game Mechanics*, https://doi.org/10.1007/978-1-4842-8873-3_1

- Novelty
- Creativity
- Achievement
- Social interaction

Novelty

Games help us escape the monotony of daily life. Most games are filled with a variety of unpredictable scenarios and content. With every new level that is unlocked, and with every turn taken while exploring the game world, there is something different to be discovered. This can be a delightful experience for the player. In open-world games like The Outer Worlds and those in the Fallout Series, you encounter unique monsters and enemies such as raiders, ferocious animals, and zombies while walking through the wasteland. You can choose to defeat them in hopes of receiving valuable items and gaining experience, or you can avoid them and try to get away. As the game progresses, you can uncover exotic locations, new NPCs (non-playable characters), and hidden treasures.

Storytelling is another essential aspect of player immersion and engagement, especially in action-adventure games. Such games are built around the stories that they tell and have mechanics that often depend on the narrative. Things like the quests you receive, the way you interact with the game's characters, and the way your character develops all depend on the storyline. The stories in a game give you the chance to live the life of make-believe characters, showing you what it feels like to step into someone else's shoes. The things they see, the places they explore, and the emotions they feel stay with you long after finishing the game.

Moreover, the prospect of living and breathing the impossible (think aliens, mythical creatures, time-travel, space battles) is quite appealing to many players, as is the chance to experience something new in every game. For example, games like Detroit: Become Human, Heavy Rain, and The Walking Dead series are story-driven and have plots that are entirely based on the player's choices. They have multiple branching storylines and endings that can only be unlocked by performing certain actions in the game.

Many games have chance-based elements that keep you on your toes. In fantasy role-playing tabletop games such as ***Dungeons and Dragons***, ***Call of Cthulhu***, ***Warhammer Fantasy Roleplay***, and ***Pathfinder***, the outcome of the dice roll determines whether you are successful in casting a spell, climbing a wall, or hiding in the forest. Similarly, ***The Hitchhiker's Guide to the Galaxy***, ***Zork***, and ***AI Dungeon*** are text adventure games in which the path that you choose to take decides how the game unfolds. You can type text in the interface, as shown in Figure 1-1, to perform certain actions in the game such as turning on a light, exiting a room, or searching for items that you need.

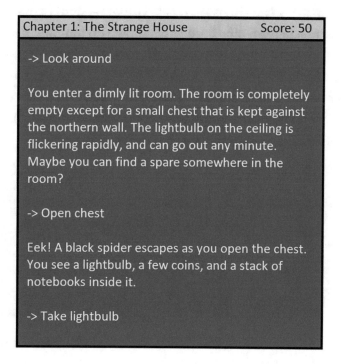

Figure 1-1. *A text-adventure style gaming interface (Created by the author)*

The randomness and luck-based aspect of these games create suspense for the players, motivating them to keep playing in anticipation of what's next. The desire for suspense goes hand-in-hand with one's creative instinct.

Creativity

Through games, we can express ourselves freely without the fear of judgment. Every game with a role-playing element supports character customization (as seen in Figure 1-2), where we can typically choose its gender, body shape, face structure, eye and eyebrow color, hair shape and color, clothes, and accessories. In games like those in the **Sims** franchise, we can also change a character's voice, personality traits, goals, and aspirations. We can choose to create virtual versions of ourselves or build an entirely new identity based on our own dreams and desires. The persona we create can be an extension of ourselves, and is the perfect opportunity for self-expression. In a lot of games with player-choice, you can choose to be the hero and save the day, or choose to be the villain and ruin it, and won't be held accountable for either path taken. This gives us the ultimate freedom – the choice to be who we want to be!

Figure 1-2. *Choosing various outfits and accessories (Designed by the author)*

In sandbox games like **Minecraft**, you can craft many different items with the resources you collect by hacking away at the pixelated game world. For example, you can cut down an oak tree (by punching it), create planks from the wood you get, and use them to create wooden pickaxes, swords, or shovels. You can build houses, mountains, and even bridges. In fact, the look of the game world is completely in your hands. This is also possible in games like **No Man's Sky**, where you can dig into the ground on any planet, changing its terrain as you wish.

There are no limits to your imagination when it comes to games that let you build things, especially simulation titles. In the theme park management game **Roller Coaster Tycoon**, you can build shops, roller coasters and other rides, footpaths, and decorative items in a given space of land. It gives you a chance to get creative with how many structures you want to build and how you want to place them. You can create gentle rides like merry-go-rounds, thrilling water rides, and even extremely intense roller coasters with lots of loops and steep drops. Based on your creation, the game simulates conditions such as the ride speed and intensity, cleanliness of the park (the virtual guests will litter the park), the number of guests that visit, and their happiness level. Since every aspect of the theme park is up to you, every player's design will be a unique masterpiece!

Achievement

Why do we do anything? Everything that we do in life, such as studying, giving an exam, or even working in a job, we do for a sense of achievement and fulfillment. Every game presents us with different kinds of challenges we need to overcome. Successfully completing these gives us a dopamine rush, motivating us to keep playing the game. Whenever we get a reward such as coins or points, it makes us want to come back to the game for more.

Many games involve talking to NPCs (non-playable characters) to receive quests and missions, then interacting with the game environment to find and use various items needed to complete them. As you go further into the game, you unlock new locations (such as the one shown in Figure 1-3) and abilities. With every task that we complete, we feel a deep sense of satisfaction at achieving something. As each level gets progressively more difficult, we feel more content on beating one that is tougher than the last one.

Figure 1-3. *A Fantasy-themed location (Created by the author on ArtBreeder)*

Finally defeating that difficult boss after the tenth try or getting the timing correct on that jump and other such moments of frustration evaporate on reaching the goal you've worked so hard for. In fact, leveling up in the game can make you feel stronger and more invincible in front of others. Making a mistake or failing in the game is usually not a big deal, as you can always start over. These losses that you sustain are much less significant than what you may experience in the real world, giving you more self-confidence. Moreover, the safety net of being able to save your progress and restore it whenever you want gives you a great sense of control.

Social Interaction

Although most games can be played independently, a lot of them allow you to meet, play with, and form genuine connections with others. You can walk around the game world, visiting places such as a marketplace or an inn (as shown in Figure 1-4) and chat freely with other players doing the same, as well as with NPCs. You can trade items, ask for help when completing a quest, or even have entire conversations with someone. In some cases, you may need to collaborate with other players to finish a certain part of the game.

Most RPGs (role-playing games) feature a PvP (Player vs. Player) combat mode where you can fight or compete with other players in-game. For example, in the game *Runescape*, you can enter an area called the wilderness to fight with others that are at a similar combat level as you for a chance to receive rare items and valuable loot. You can also trade items that you might need to train a skill or to complete a quest.

Oftentimes, on the other side of the screen is an entire gaming community that is built in and around the game. You can get up, turn on your computer or phone, and jump into a game to find a whole world of people that you can potentially form enduring friendships with!

Figure 1-4. *A pixel-based fantasy RPG inn (Source: Super Retro World Asset pack by Gif,* `https://twitter.com/gif_not_jif`*)*

Rules That Are Fun to Follow

Behind every game is a set of rules and objectives that guide the player and lead to hours of enjoyable gameplay – a concept called Game Mechanics. They can be incredibly simple, as in the case of the famous ***Flappy Bird*** game – where you simply have to tap the screen at the right time to make the bird bounce against gravity and pass through the gaps between an endless series of pipes, as depicted in Figure 1-5. The further you go, the higher your score will be.

Game mechanics can also be more diverse, as in the case of classic platformers like ***Super Mario Bros.*** or ***Sonic the Hedgehog***, where you can jump on top of the monsters to defeat them and collect power-ups that give special abilities to your character.

Fun Fact   The game *Flappy Bird* was quite popular, receiving more than 50 million downloads and generating a profit of over $50,000 per day for its creator, Dong Nguyen. But it became so addictive to its players that he decided to completely remove it from mobile app stores!

Just like an artist who paints a picture according to an artistic vision, game developers use their imagination to come up with challenges and ways for the player to enjoy playing the game. In the following pages, we will learn how to develop interesting game mechanics and learn from the ones used in popular games.

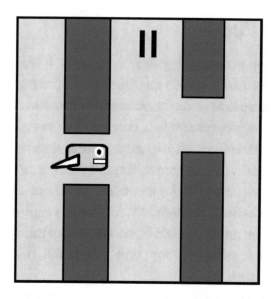

Figure 1-5. *Author's depiction of the game Flappy Bird*

Appeal of Different Game Genres

In the world of games, there is something for everyone – from short, simple, casual games that you can play on your mobile to pass the time to mass multiplayer online role-playing games (MMORPGs) with realistic graphics, immersive scenarios, and complex storylines that will keep you immersed for hours at a time. Just as books and movies have different genres, such as Action, Thriller, Romance, Comedy, Sci-fi, and Drama, games can also be classified into different groups based on the player interaction and gameplay. Every video game broadly falls under one or more of these categories – Casual and Puzzle, Strategy and Simulation, Action-Adventure, and Role-Playing.

Casual and Puzzle

Open a mobile app store on any given day, and you'll see millions, sometimes billions of downloads on some of the most popular games in this genre. These types of games are created for those who want some simple, mindless entertainment for a short while. They are perfect for those who don't necessarily want to spend a lot of time dealing with the depth and complexity of AAA games. You can pick one up whenever you have pockets of free time and play it virtually anywhere – while waiting for the bus, traveling to work, watching TV, or even at a gathering or party. In fact, you don't need any special skills, knowledge, or much effort to play; all you need is a few minutes of your time. Due to this, people of all ages are drawn to play such games.

Most of these have colorful, attractive graphics that promise you a great experience. Usually being free to play, they let you purchase special items or characters using your credit card. They often offer points, new levels, extra lives, or in-game boosts in exchange for watching a short video advertisement (mostly of other casual games!). Moreover, they also give you attractive rewards for returning to play every day. This keeps players engaged and coming back for more. Moreover, certain types of games, called "hyper-casual," usually don't even need to be downloaded. In fact, a lot of them can be played in the browser or within another App, and are often integrated with social networking sites. People usually play them for short-term entertainment, instant gratification, and social interaction.

The game mechanics involved in casual games are usually very easy to understand and include combinations of taps, swipes, or clicks on the screen. Let's take a look at some famous examples:

- **Subway Surfers**

  You play a character called Jake, who is being chased by a guard and his dog down a set of train tracks. Just like in many other endless runner games, the character runs automatically and collects coins along the way. You can swipe left or right to switch lanes, swipe upwards for jumping, and swipe down to crouch under hurdles. With the help of a slope on certain trains, you can climb and run on top of them, or even soar above them using a jetpack that randomly spawns.

  There are various other power-ups you can collect and use for special boosts and effects – a pogo stick or super sneakers for jumping high into the sky lined with coins and other collectibles, a coin magnet that automatically attracts nearby coins, a score multiplier that increases the score at a faster rate, and a hoverboard that protects you from crashing for a few seconds.

  You can use the coins that you collect on the train tracks to buy new characters, outfits, accessories, and power-ups. The game gets faster and more challenging the longer you run and ends as soon as you hit an obstacle such as a train or a hurdle (unless you've activated a hoverboard). You can use the collectible key token or watch an advertisement to continue playing the game, without having to restart it.

- **Cut the Rope**

  In this game, you have to feed a piece of candy to a character called Om Nom. The challenge here is that the candy is attached to one or more pieces of a rope, and you need to cut it in a certain way such that the rope swings and the candy falls perfectly into the character's mouth, as shown in Figure 1-6. The place where you make the cut as well as the timing of your cuts determines how fast and in which direction the rope swings. If you cut the rope such that the candy doesn't fall into Om Nom's mouth, you lose the level and need to start over.

  There are many games in the *Cut the Rope* series, each with different themes, graphics, and features. Most versions have been downloaded more than 50 million times! The original version of the game is packed with many exciting game mechanics that are unique to every set of levels (called a "box").

  Each box introduces new gameplay elements and has a certain number of levels. For instance, the first one, called the "Cardboard Box," has bubbles that can make the candy float upwards, automatic ropes that attach to the candy when it comes close to them, and spikes that can break the candy. Another one called the "Magic Box" features Magic Hats that teleport the candy from one hat to another. You need a certain number of stars to unlock a new Box, which you can collect in every level. The fact that there are tons of unique boxes loaded with so many game mechanics means that there is always something new to experience when playing this game. This makes this franchise extremely popular when it comes to mobile gaming.

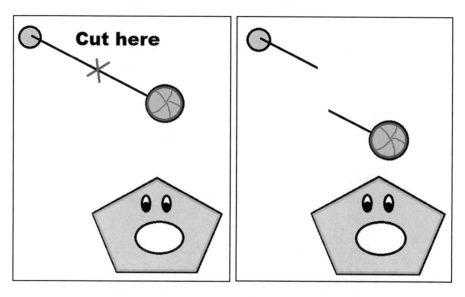

Figure 1-6. *Author's depiction of the game Cut the Rope, where you have to cut the rope to make the candy fall into the character's mouth*

- **Homescapes**

  You play as a Butler who has returned to his childhood home that is in dire need of renovation. The main gameplay is similar to **Candy Crush**, except that instead of matching candy, you have to create matching sets of books, lamps, ribbons, and teacups in a limited number of turns. You get a total of five lives at a time, and each matching game consumes one of these lives.

The game grants stars for successfully completing a level that you can use for activities like calling someone on the phone, buying furniture, setting up a TV, changing the wallpaper and carpets in a room, or even decorating the garden. You are usually given three choices for every furniture, structure, or decorative element (such as the wallpaper or flooring), such as the ones shown in Figure 1-7. From time to time, the game also rewards you with infinite lives or special power-ups that last for a short period of time for reaching certain goals. As lives are rare in the game (you need to wait for 30 minutes for each of them to get refilled) and power-ups are hard to come by (they need to be earned), the player doesn't want to "miss out" on these free gifts, and ends up playing for a longer period of time!

Just like in **Candy Crush**, the starting levels are easy to beat, which gives you the impression that you are really good at the game, but the subsequent levels keep getting progressively difficult. This keeps things from getting boring, but might make the game more frustrating for players.

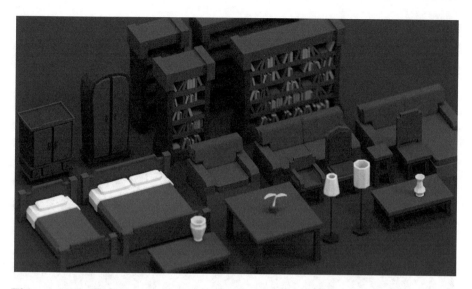

Figure 1-7. *You can customize the furniture in some casual games like Homescapes (Source: Ultimate Furniture Pack, LowPoly Models by @Quaternius)*

Strategy and Simulation

Games open up doorways to virtual worlds that often mimic or simulate real-world elements. Want to fly an airplane over cities, forests, mountains, and mesmerizing landscapes? Want to drive across Europe in a truck while exploring its cities and roads? It's all possible in games like ***Microsoft's Flight Simulator*** and ***Euro Truck Simulator 2***. They place you in highly detailed, immersive real-world environments that make you lose touch with reality, if only for a short while, which is quite enticing for many players.

In base-building games, you can build the world of your dreams and decide what happens in them. Such games give you the power to change the world in any way you see fit, by adding roads, buildings, parks, and even modifying the landscape by raising or lowering terrain to create mountains and valleys. The basic idea behind any base-building game is the same. With every resource you collect, you can create tools, develop buildings and fascinating structures (as shown in Figure 1-8), and advance the technology in your world.

Figure 1-8. *Base-building games let you create beautiful structures (Source: Medieval Village Pack, LowPoly Models by @Quaternius)*

Many games start out by giving you a set of mini goals that you have to achieve to progress further in the game. For instance, you might need to create defense posts, build essential shops, or develop basic services like providing power and water to your world's virtual inhabitants. Games like these are so addictive that players often spend days, months, or even years playing them.

In almost all strategy games, every small decision you make can lead to your imminent victory or defeat. The weight of this responsibility provides just the right amount of stress needed for optimal critical thinking. If a player gets the desired result after hours of gameplay, it can lead to an amazing gameplay experience. If not, the player often has the choice to go back a few steps by loading previous saved versions of the game or even start fresh from the beginning for a second chance at victory.

It can be extremely satisfying for one to see the end product they have created – an impenetrable fortress base, a thriving restaurant, hospital or theme park, or a highly advanced civilization. Let's take a look at some famous games in this genre:

- **Clash of Clans**

    With more than 500 million downloads, this is one of the most popular base-building games out there on the market. You play as the chief of a village who has to turn the given piece of land into a fortified base. You can get the resources needed by producing them in your village, attacking other players' villages, or purchasing them with the help of medals earned during battle. You have to train troops that include characters with different abilities such as Barbarians, Giants, Archers, Wizards, and Dragons, among many, many others.

    Different structures such as a Builder's Hut, Gold Mine, Gold Storage, and defense towers need to be constructed to strengthen your base against raids by other players. Once you're ready, you can search for another player's base to attack, deploy your troops to their base, and sit back and watch the battle take place automatically. Your soldiers will hack away at the enemy structures, and you usually end up losing some of them during the process. You also get rewards after the battle according to your performance, which you can then use to upgrade your base and troops even more.

There are different in-game currencies, namely, Gold, Elixir, and Gems, which can help you buy resources, upgrade your troops and buildings, and speed up the completion of certain activities in the game. Gems can be bought with real-world money, and a lot of hardcore players spend hundreds of dollars to buy them, as well as to purchase various season passes that offer exclusive items and upgrades.

The game is based on a persistent world that keeps developing when you're away from it, and there are always new updates that developers release from time to time. Because of this, you can potentially play Clash of Clans for years!

- **Age of Empires**

This award-winning franchise consists of a number of iconic real-time strategy games that are based on historical events. You get the chance to create an Empire based on one of many civilizations such as the Aztecs, Byzantines, Mayans, Goths, Mongols, Huns, and Persians, each of which has unique skills, bonuses, and technology. For instance, Aztec villagers can carry more resources at a time, Byzantine fire ships can attack faster, and Persian Town Centers and Docks have more HP or Hitpoints (which makes them harder to destroy by the enemy). In these games, you start off living in the Stone Age with a handful of villagers and a simple Townhall. The goal is to advance through different technological ages, that is, times of innovation, such as the Stone Age, Tool Age, Bronze Age, and

Iron Age. As you progress through them, you unlock newer and better tools, technology, weapons, and units (such as cavalry, swordsmen, catapults, war elephants, boats and ships).

Most of the game map is unrevealed, and you need to explore it in order to discover resources such as Berry bushes that can be foraged for food, rocks that can mined for ores, trees that can be cut down for wood, and animals that you can hunt for food. The more villagers you assign to a certain resource, the faster it can be gathered. These resources, in turn, help advance your civilization, as you use them to create walls, watch towers, farms, houses, castles, military units, markets, ships and boats, various buildings (as shown in Figure 1-9), and more villagers.

Figure 1-9. *Creating houses, castles, walls, farms, and other structures in a base-building game (Source: Ultimate Fantasy RTS Pack by Quaternius)*

As you explore the map, you come across other civilizations that are in different stages of progress, which are your competitors in the game. You can win the game through conquest (destroying all enemy units and buildings), capturing and defending an artifact or a ruin for 2000 in-game years, or building a Wonder (a special massive structure that is the pride of your civilization) that can stand for 2000 in-game years.

Fun Fact   Age of Empires has a long-standing, 25-year legacy, spanning over five major titles with a number of spin-offs, and has over 25 million copies sold. Every new version added new civilizations, gameplay modes, maps, and improved graphics and mechanics.

- **Fallout Shelter**

    In this game, you are in charge of building and managing a state-of-the-art underground vault beneath a highly radioactive world. As its overseer, you have to build different types of resource-generating rooms such as for power generation, food and medicine production, and water treatment.

    From time to time, new explorers arrive at the door of your vault, and you can let them in and assign them to these rooms. These dwellers level up over time and can be equipped with weapons and items to carry out different kinds of tasks. You can also assign a male and a female dweller to the Living Quarter room to "breed" new dwellers by producing babies.

The happiness of your dwellers is in your hands, as it depends on how effectively you gather resources in the game. You need to make sure that you don't run out of power, food, and electricity, which are all produced slowly over time in various vault rooms. It's possible to "rush" the production in any room, either risk-free by watching a video advertisement, or at a risk of triggering an incident such as a vault fire or a radroach (radioactive cockroach) infestation in the room being rushed. If such an incident happens in a room, the dwellers in that room try to fight it off or get rid of it.

You can earn "caps" (bottle caps), the game's main currency, by completing various objectives such as "Successfully extinguish 3 Vault Fires," and spend them on upgrading your vault and its dwellers. Players sometimes receive a special item called a "lunchbox" as a reward, which is filled with goodies such as new dwellers, advanced gear, and essential items. As these help you progress in the game much faster, a lot of players choose to buy them through microtransactions.

Action-Adventure

The focus on speed, timing, and precision of gameplay makes action-adventure games exciting to play. A lot of the retro arcade games such as *Super Mario Bros.*, *Sonic the Hedgehog*, *Pac-man*, *Space Invaders*, and *Donkey Kong* are famous for their flashy pixel graphics and upbeat 8-bit music soundtracks. When people play these vintage classics today, it evokes a strong feeling of nostalgia within them. For many who have grown up playing or hearing about these games, replaying them makes them feel like a kid again, where they can forget about their worries and responsibilities for a short time.

There are many sub-genres that fall under the category of Action-adventure. Fighting game titles such as **Street Fighter**, **Mortal Kombat**, **Tekken**, and **Super Smash Bros.** have incredibly fast-paced, one-on-one combat. In most of these games, you play as one of two characters fighting each other in a certain location such as the street, mountainside, temple, beach, or forest. Using your character's unique abilities to defeat the opponent, you can throw punches and kicks, jump in the air, and make special power moves. The objective is to knock out the other player while defending your own. Every time you replay a match, you get a chance to practice and improve your skills. Figure 1-10 shows an example of a fighting game.

Figure 1-10. *An intense one-on-one player battle in a fighting game (Source: Streets of Fight Asset Pack by Ansimuz)*

Platformer games all have the same basic idea behind them – walk, run, jump on, or fly across platforms while collecting trinkets like coins, quest items, keys, power-ups, and extra lives. Most of them are developed based on complex in-game physics that make Player movements and reactions smooth and realistic. Early platformers like **Donkey Kong** and **Super Mario Bros.** focused more on jumping, climbing, collecting, shooting, and avoiding falling obstacles; later ones like **Celeste**, **Hollow Knight**, and **Super Meat Boy** have you performing stunts and performing complex attacks. Figure 1-11 shows a futuristic platformer with a robot as the player.

Figure 1-11. *A simple platformer with a futuristic robot player (Source: Mega Bot Areas and Megabot Asset Packs by Ansimuz)*

First Person Shooter (FPS) games place you in the proverbial shoes of the protagonist, giving you the chance to see the game world through their eyes. Third Person Shooters are similar to FPS, the only difference being that you can see the character that you are controlling. Both of these pose the challenge of mastering the character's movements while avoiding or shooting at enemies, which can be thrilling for the player. As these games are usually fast paced and unpredictable from moment to moment, they test your muscle memory, reflexes, as well as problem-solving skills.

In all action-adventure games, you need to make instant decisions in a short timing window to move smoothly throughout the game level. Quickly tapping a key or a button within a few seconds can mean the difference between falling off the edge of a cliff and having to start over the game, or successfully making it across a large gap when jumping. Moreover, the visuals, sound effects, and storyline make games in this genre highly appealing and exhilarating to play. Let's take a look at some popular examples:

- **Tomb Raider**

   This ultimate adventure franchise has tons of games such as the original 1996 ***Tomb Raider***, ***Curse of the Sword***, ***The Prophecy***, ***Legend***, ***Anniversary***, and ***Shadow of the Tomb Raider***, among others. In all these games, you play as Lara Croft, a highly intelligent, rich, athletic British archaeologist who travels to mysterious places in search of relics, artifacts, and historical secrets. Being a treasure hunter and a tomb raider, you get to explore exotic locations such as Peru, Bolivia, Ghana, Cambodia, and Siberia.

   You often find yourself in the trickiest situations – stuck in a dark crevice with nothing but your flashlight to guide you, balancing precariously on a wooden bridge swinging because of wind, or falling into a snake pit full of hissing cobras.

   Playing in the third person view, you get the chance to perform incredible stunts such as walking on the edge of a cliff, jumping and grabbing a ledge, and swinging on branches with the help of a grappling hook. Every time you attempt such a stunt, there are grunting, shouting, and cursing sound effects that makes it seem like the character is actually making a lot of effort. You also get the chance to fight monsters like jaguars, giant lizards, dinosaurs, and other mythical creatures.

There is a lot of puzzle-solving that you need to do in these games, especially in recent ones like the Shadow of the Tomb Raider. For instance, you might need to find a way to fill a bucket to pull down a lever that it's attached to, escape a room full of lava by laying down a stone bridge or find a path to a hidden city. From spiked moving walls that close in on you, to animals that jump at you out of nowhere, and even to hidden levers that open secret doors, there are lots of fascinating mechanics in these games.

- **The Outer Worlds**

In this futuristic, space-themed FPS game, you are awakened from cryogenic sleep on a colonist ship that is headed for the farthest reaches of the galaxy. After a cinematic cut scene, the game starts off with the character creation screen. You can choose some of your attributes such as your Strength, Intelligence, Perception, Charm, and Temperament, and how good or bad you are at certain skills such as persuasion and intimidation, defense, stealth, and engineering. You can do this by spending a certain number of points (you are given some at the beginning of the game), which you will earn more of every time you level up. The combination of your attributes and skills determines the outcome of certain events in the game. For example, to intimidate someone in the game during a dialog, you need a certain number of points assigned to this ability.

This game has many notable mechanics such as Tactical Time Dilation (TTD), which slows down time, allowing you to aim and shoot accurately at enemies. Once you use this ability, you need to wait for the TTD meter to fill up again before using it. Another interesting mechanic is the holographic shroud, which makes you invisible for a short period of time.

The main gameplay revolves around running around on alien planets collecting food, medicine, gear, and other items, and interacting with the NPCs. Talking to them will give you quests that you can complete to gain favor with certain "factions" in the game, while performing activities like stealing or trespassing will hurt your reputation. The whole idea of the game is based on the fact that your decisions will have consequences, and will, ultimately, affect how the game story unfolds.

- **Immortals Fenyx Rising**

In this mythological adventure game, you play as Fenyx, a mortal (human) who is trying to stop the Greek monster Typhon from destroying the world by restoring the lost power of ancient Greek gods such as Aphrodite, Athena, Ares, and Hephaestus (through various quests). As Fenyx's brother and other countless other mortals have been turned to stone, it is up to Fenyx alone to save them by defeating Typhon. There are various interesting cut scenes in the game that show the story as it progresses, and the entire thing is hilariously narrated by Zeus (who cracks jokes and engages in a back-and-forth banter with a chained Titan called Prometheus).

This game has a *"The Legend of Zelda: Breath of the Wild"* feel to it, as your character gets to run around a large open world, exploring it while fighting monsters and solving puzzles. Every major area of the world has a distinctive look and feel to it, and is filled with unique structures and challenges. You can climb cliffs or massive statues, fly or glide across short distances (with your wings of Daedalus), and even ride a mount (such as a horse or a deer). These actions consume stamina, which needs to be recharged by staying on the ground from time to time.

You also have a number of interesting unlockable abilities called "Godly Powers" that can be used in battle, such as Herakles' Strength (lets you lift and throw large boulders), Athena's Dash (lets you boost forward and damage things in your path), and Hephaistos' Hammer (summons a massive hammer that can be slammed on the ground to damage and knock back enemies). An interesting mechanic in this game is the Apollo's Arrow, whose trajectory can be controlled by the player after being shot.

The game has a number of special arenas called the
Vaults of Tartaros that the player has to complete.
Every vault has a number of action-packed puzzles
that you need to solve, such as by rolling a ball onto
a floor switch or flying and gliding across large
gaps between platforms. If you fall off any of the
platforms in these vaults, you suffer some damage,
and restart from the last checkpoint. The vaults are
also filled with hidden chests filled with unique gear
(that can be easily missed and are more challenging
to reach), and sometimes ferocious enemies that
need to be defeated.

Role-Playing Games (RPGs)

Video games give us a chance to live out situations that we might never get
to experience in real life. We can fight dragons, climb mountains, or even
travel light years to alien galaxies, all from the comfort of our homes. Role-
playing games feature amazing, meticulously designed game worlds based
on themes such as Post-apocalyptic, Medieval, Historical, or Outer Space.

There is always something new to discover, someplace new to explore,
and interesting people to meet. In addition, the hyperrealistic characters
(as shown in Figure 1-12) and places can blur the lines between fantasy
and reality. Our brain is tricked into imagining that what we see on the
screen is actually happening in real life. This is especially true in the case
of ultra-famous titles like Fallout, Uncharted, and Cyberpunk 2077.

Figure 1-12. *Hyperrealistic characters can blur the lines between reality and fiction (Created by the author on Artbreeder)*

Some games that fall under the Mass Multiplayer Online Role Playing Games (MMORPGs) category such as ***World of Warcraft***, ***RuneScape***, and ***Lost Ark*** have tens of millions of total players. These have entire websites, wiki pages, YouTube channels, Twitch channels, and Discord servers dedicated to them, telling you everything you might want to know about the game. What makes them so popular? One simple idea – the ability to become a new person and live a completely different life in a universe that can only exist in our imagination. Moreover, RPGs let you socialize and interact with players all over the world, take part in missions and quests with them and even fight against them. A lot of players play these games for years, spending more time in virtual worlds than on real-world activities. Let's take a look at some interesting game mechanics used in a few famous RPG games:

- **Old School RuneScape**

  In this fantasy-themed, retro-styled game, the fictional realm of Gielinor is your playground. You can fish for lobsters and sharks, cook edible food items like pizzas, cakes, and pies, or even fight mythical monsters like goblins, dragons, and giants. You can trade items with other players and chat with them in the game, and even buy and sell valuable items on the in-game marketplace called the Grand Exchange. There are over 150+ story-rich quests filled with *Runescape* lore that you can complete in the game (which can take hours or even days) with the help of these items, and by wearing certain gear. All the quests have certain requirements, and the more advanced ones can only be unlocked when you have achieved a specific level in a skill or when you have completed certain other quests. In fact, there are 23 different skills that you can train, such as Attack, Mining, Defense, Agility, Smithing, Magic, Woodcutting, Farming, Herblore, Cooking, and Fishing. Each of these skills takes more time to train the higher the level you are in it. For example, it might take you a few minutes to train cooking for the first 4–5 levels, but it can take months to train the same skill from level 95 to 99 (the last few levels).

Once you enter into combat with an enemy, you both attack each other alternately, and cause a random amount of damage each time; the higher your combat level, the more the possibility of a larger hit value on every game tick. After each fight, you will gain experience in certain skills such as Attack, Strength, Hitpoint level, and Defense. There are three different modes of combat such as Melee, Ranged, and Magic and each of them has specific equipment, which, if worn, gives a bonus to the player.

Players that take the pay-to-play path in this game have a great advantage in training skills and combat, and a lot of people choose to pay for membership for this reason. They also have access to a greater portion of the game map, can complete a lot more quests, and have significantly better and more expensive armor and gear available than free-to-play members. Due to this exclusivity of certain content, players feel the "fear of missing out" and are motivated to pay for more. Players of both modes of the game feel a great sense of achievement because of the game's intuitive leveling-up model of gameplay.

- **The Elder Scrolls V: Skyrim**

  The fifth installment in the fantasy role-playing *Elder Scrolls* series, this is one of Bethesda Game Studio's most popular releases to date. It features a vast open world that you can explore while choosing to complete quests, attacking NPCs or just wandering around and discovering new places in the game's highly detailed world. At the beginning of the game, you can pick the "race" of your character. Each of the ten possible races has unique characteristics and abilities, such as a certain skill they excel at or the spells that they can cast. Some examples of races include:

  - **Nord** – Being the human citizens of Skyrim, they are great warriors who are incredibly resistant to cold and have the ability to make opponents flee with a battlecry.

- **Khajiit** – These are feline-faced beasts that are known for their agility, stealth, intelligence, and night vision. This makes them excellent thieves, assassins, and warriors.

- **Bretons** – Having a mixture of human and elven ancestry, they have high magic resistance and are great mages with the ability to absorb spells.

- **Argonians** – They look like reptiles, and make brilliant thieves, scouts, and ambushers due to their stealth and lockpicking abilities.

There are tons of skills such as Smithing, Heavy Armor, Two-Handed or One-Handed (Weapon wielding), Pickpocket, Alchemy, Illusion, Conjuration, and Restoration, from a range of 15 to 25 (the higher the better). Every race has a certain skill that they have the highest level in. For example, the Altmer or the High Elf race is the best at the Illusion, which lets you cast various spells such as "Calm" that potentially stops an enemy from attacking for 30 seconds, and "Courage" that prevents an enemy from fleeing for 60 seconds, while giving you extra stamina and health.

In the game, you can join several different groups or factions, the leaders of which assign you tasks or quests. There are certain conditions (in the form of quest completion) that allow you to join a certain faction (such as slaying a dragon or clearing a fort of bandits that are occupying it), and those that prevent you from entering it. All in all, Skyrim is considered to be a masterpiece that gives its players immense freedom to explore an amazing open world while creating unique character builds.

- **Stardew Valley**

This is a simulation role-playing game in which you play as a character who inherits their grandfather's land and develops it into the farm of their dreams. In this top-down pixel-art-based game, you can run around gaining experience in a number of skills that include Farming, Mining, Foraging, Fishing, and Combat. Starting at 0, you can reach a level of up to 10 in each, with unique perks at every level. You can also interact with the NPCs who each have their own personalities and quirks. It's also possible to date various NPCs and start a family with them!

One unique mechanic in this game is the presence of four different seasons – spring, summer, fall, and winter. During each one, the game's resources, which you can forage, keep changing to keep things new and fresh. For example, in the spring you can collect Daffodils and Dandelions, and in the summer, Sweet Pea and Spice Berry. Even the fish in the lakes also change according to the time of the day, the season, and the location. Due to this, it takes quite a lot of effort to find all types of fish in the game as well as to progress the fishing skill.

Figure 1-13.   A pixel game scene similar to Stardew Valley (Credit: Super Retro World Asset pack by Gif, https://twitter.com/gif_ not_jif)

Fun Fact   Stardew Valley was a solo project, designed entirely by an Indie developer Eric Barone within a period of four years. He taught himself all the skills needed to create the game, handcrafting every aspect including the art, music, programming, and the design. The game gained almost instant success a few months after its release, and has sold over 20 million copies across all gaming platforms.

Overall, this game has a great amount of depth and a lot of great, relaxing content that players can spend their time on. A pixel game scene similar to **Stardew Valley** can be seen in Figure 1-13.

Key Takeaways

In this chapter, we saw how players look for novelty, creativity, achievement, and social interaction, whenever they pick up a game. We also took a look at key game mechanics and tactics of engagement used in:

- Casual and Puzzle titles – Subway Surfers, Cut the Rope, Homescapes

- Strategy and Simulation titles – Age of Empires, Clash of Clans, Fallout Shelter

- Action-Adventure games – Tomb Raider, The Outer Worlds, Immortal Fenyx Rising

- Role-Playing (RPG) games – Old School RuneScape, The Elder Scrolls V: Skyrim, and Stardew Valley

CHAPTER 2

Creating Fun Gameplay

In this chapter, we'll dive into the key elements of gameplay. We will understand the types of choices that exist in Player-Choice-based games and will learn how to create meaningful ones. We will also learn about game balancing and the importance of having in-game tutorials. Finally, we'll briefly discuss the impact of storytelling and the game narrative on the player experience.

Making Choices That Matter

Sid Meier, the creator of the popular turn-based strategy game *Civilization*, once said, "Games are a series of interesting decisions." This is particularly true in the case of player-choice-based games. In many such games, the smallest of actions can have the potential to alter the course of the entire game. Seeing the game unfold after making certain decisions gives players a sense of agency and control over a make-believe world.

© Maithili Dhule 2022
M. Dhule, *Exploring Game Mechanics*, https://doi.org/10.1007/978-1-4842-8873-3_2

A choice is meaningful for players if they can see its consequences in the game. Gamers usually have to face many different types of decisions[1] in games, such as:

- **The Hollow Decision** – has no major impact on the game

- **The Obvious Decision** – there is a certain clear path to follow

- **The Uninformed Decision** – is random, to some extent

- **The Informed Decision** – is well thought-out

- **The Immediate Decision** – is an instant or one that requires quick thinking

- **The Weighted Decision** – in which, every path has consequences

- **The Moral Decision** – there is a dilemma between right or wrong

- **The Long-Term Decision** – impacts a large part of the game

Let's take a look at each of them.

The Hollow Decision

This type of decision is based purely on the individual player's preference or randomness in the game. As a result, there are no real consequences on the gameplay. Every game that supports character customization lets you pick how your character looks and the outfits and accessories it wears, which are merely aesthetics that enhance your gaming experience.

The Obvious Decision

Sometimes, games give us the impression that we are free to choose any path that we want while compelling us to pick and follow a certain one. In the game **Subway Surfers**, for example, you have a very simple choice to make at every single moment in the game – whether to keep running in your current lane or switch tracks to avoid hitting obstacles. Sometimes, two out of the three tracks are blocked by trains, hurdles, or tunnel walls. To dodge these obstacles, you are forced to run on the third one that's open; an obvious decision you make to avoid losing the game! This is shown in Figure 2-1.

Figure 2-1. *The obvious path is the one that's clear from obstacles (Source: Designed by pch.vector on Freepik)*

The Uninformed Decision

If you have limited information on how the game will turn out when making a relatively random choice, chances are, you're making an uninformed decision. The popular game of ***Rock-Paper-Scissors***, as shown in Figure 2-2, is an excellent example. In every round, each player holds out either their fist (rock), flat palm (paper), or index and middle fingers (scissors). Winning or losing is based on a simple concept – rock defeats scissors, scissors defeat paper, and paper defeats rock. Another great example of uninformed decision-making is seen in the game **Pokémon Go**. There are many different types of Pokémon in the game, such as Fire, Water, Grass, Electric, Ice, etc. Before the start of any battle, you have to choose 3 Pokémon from your collection, and your opponent does the same. Since you have no way to know the ones your opponent has selected, winning or losing the game all depends on how effective or stronger your Pokémon turn out to be against those of your opponent.

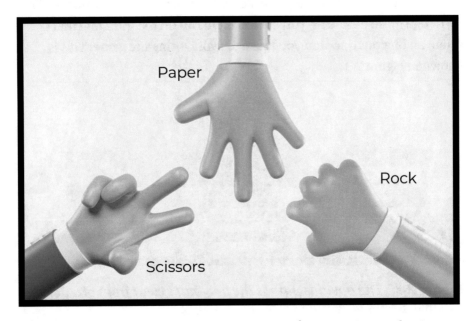

Figure 2-2. *A game of Rock-Paper-Scissors (Source: Created using image designed by DilokaStudio on Freepik)*

The Informed Decision

In this type of decision-making, you can see some of the effects that your decisions will have on the game beforehand, giving you plenty of time to think and make your choices. Racing games like **Forza Horizon 5**, **Gran Turismo 7**, and **Automation** have extremely detailed car customization options. You can control the visual aspects of the car such as its style, model, paint color, and decals, (Figure 2-3 shows an example of two cars with different paint jobs that can be chosen in a racing game). Moreover, you can also customize other functional aspects of the car such as the body components (bumpers, spoilers, and roof), the engine, braking mechanism, and even the texture of the wheel. You can then see how your customization affects the performance of your car, which includes things like the maximum speed and the ease and effectiveness of steering, braking, and acceleration.

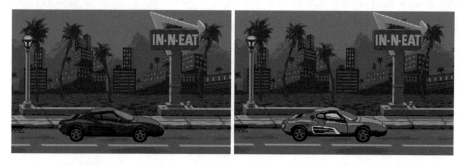

Figure 2-3. *Customizing the car in a racing game (Source: Created using artwork from the Miami Synth Asset Pack by Ansimuz)*

Fun Fact   The *Forza Horizon* games feature many hyperrealistic locations and biomes, including Urban Cities, Canyons, Farmlands, Jungles, Deserts, and Beach coasts, which are all based on real-world locations and have dynamic weather systems. The games also have tons of car models that are identical to those made by car companies, such as Audi, Mercedes-Benz, Porsche, Lamborghini, Ferrari, and Ford, among lots of others.

The Immediate Decision

Players sometimes face a situation where they need to make an instant decision that almost immediately impacts the game. For instance, in every first-person shooter (FPS) game, such as those in the **Halo**, **Call of Duty**, and **DOOM** franchises, you need to think and act fast in order to survive the chaos happening around you. Within the span of a short timing window, you need to decide whether to run, hide, dodge, shoot, or reload. Hesitate a second too long when facing an onslaught of enemies, and the game will be over before you know it.

The Weighted Decision

This is one of the hardest decisions to make in the game, as there will be pros and cons for every option that you choose. Some of these options might change the entire course of the game and can also impact how the world looks like as you progress in the game. Examples include siding with either the good or evil faction in a game (**Star Wars**), choosing to spare the lives of some characters that may later become your allies (**Witcher 3**), or even choosing to be a pacifist and avoiding fighting altogether (**Undertale**).

The Moral Decision

Many choice-based games are filled with unique moral dilemmas that the player has to face. They make you stop and think whether a certain choice in the game is morally "right" or "wrong." Examples include choosing to run away to save your own life or risking it to save someone else's (**The Walking Dead**), or stealing from another family in order to feed yours (**Life is Strange 2**).

The Long-Term Decision

Some choices you make might end up affecting a large part of your gameplay. A lot of games, for instance, let you adjust the difficulty setting at the start. Playing in a higher difficulty mode can affect the damage you deal or receive, make bosses harder to defeat and can even impact the rate at which you level up your skills and gain experience points. The game *Subnautica* features four game modes, namely, Survival, Hardcore, Freedom, and Creative. In the first two modes, you need to manage your health, oxygen, food, and water levels in order to survive. The Hardcore mode, the tougher one among the two, only gives you one life; if you die in the game, you need to start all over from the beginning. The Freedom and Creative modes are much more relaxed, letting you focus on things like building and exploration.

Designing Better Player Choices

Player choice can be one of the most powerful aspects of gameplay and can help players connect with the game. For a choice to be meaningful for a player, it should have a significant, observable impact on the game. You should give the player different types of choices that have both positive and negative consequences and vary in type and intensity, to keep things from getting boring. At the same time, you should keep in mind that forcing certain choices on the players can frustrate the player, ruining the gaming experience for them. Fast-paced, life-or-death action moments in a game should be balanced with pockets of cool-down times during which the players can stop and appreciate their achievements and get ready for the next stage.

Permanence of the Choice

Games give us a chance to freely make dangerous, risky decisions without worrying about the consequences. When presented with many options, players get the courage to choose a difficult choice or take the unknown path out of sheer curiosity as to what will happen in the game. Unlike real life, they have the safety net of going back and reloading their save file if they don't like what they see. The game *Life Is Strange* has the core gameplay mechanic of being able to "rewind time" which lets you make a choice and see its consequences and undo it and make a different one if you're not happy with the outcome. In the visual novel game *Steins; Gate*, choosing to check your phone, make a call, or send an email at certain times can lead to completely different storylines. Games like these offer multiple different endings that will decide the fate of the main characters. Let's take a look at the branching storyline of a choice-based horror game to understand how our choices can impact the game's story.

Fun Fact   The game *The Stanley Parable* is a first person exploration game in which the narrator continuously guides you to do certain actions in the game, such as opening a specific door. He comments and gives his opinion on every action you do in the game. If you ignore him, do the opposite of what he says, or spend too much time in a certain location, it leads to humorous consequences and funny commentary by the narrator.

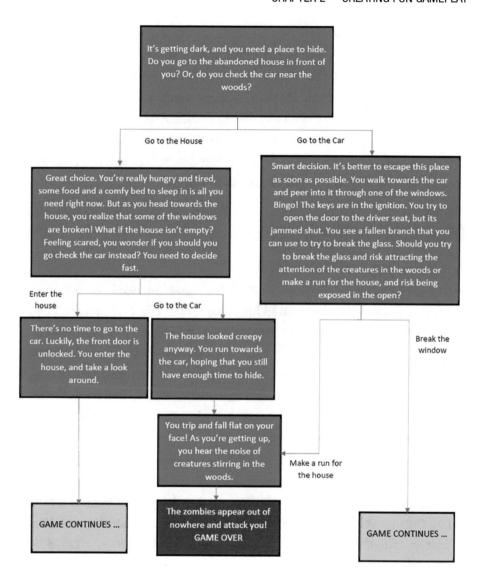

The Butterfly Effect

An important element related to chaos theory, the Butterfly Effect, states that a very minor change, for example, a butterfly flapping its wings in one part of the world, can lead to drastic and even disastrous outcomes, such as a hurricane, somewhere else. Every path that you choose to take in a choice-based game can lead to several more. Before you know it, you're experiencing one of many permutations of events possible in the game. ***Detroit: Become Human***, an action-adventure game with multiple playable characters, is an excellent example. Almost every choice you make in the game such as choosing to either peacefully talk with or forcefully intimidate a robot will change the destiny of the characters as well as the ultimate fate of the entire game world.

Maintaining the Illusion

Although games provide a semblance of freedom for the players, their actions are ultimately confined to the limited pool of possibilities that game developers have accounted for. Does it mean that true choice is an illusion since you can only perform actions that stick to a specific set of rules? Mirroring the real world, where we can only control ourselves, not the things that happen around us, games connect to the player on a deeper level when they observe and act through the characters that they control. The more time we spend in these game worlds, the more emotional attachment we feel toward the game and its characters.

A lot of games give us a vast number of reasonable choices to pick from, to such an extent that we never feel like we lack a truly free choice. By putting themselves in the player's shoes, game developers should account for all the possible scenarios and branching storylines that they want the players to experience in a choice-based game. It is important to consider the answers to questions like

- What emotions would the player feel in a particular situation?

- What is the thought process like for different kinds of players?

- Are the decisions going to impact a major part of the game?

- How many possible endings is the game going to have?

- Is the game going to be replayable (by making different choices each time)?

Developing the game based on such points can help to complete various loops in the game, leading to a wholesome gaming experience for the player.

Game Balancing

How many times have you breezed through the first few levels of a game, only to end up stuck and frustrated after a few more? Many games start out great, but if they aren't designed to sustain the "fun" element throughout, they can turn out to be terribly disappointing.

For a game to be considered fun to play, its objectives and mechanics should be clearly understood by its players. It's important that the game isn't "unfair" at any point and that it doesn't have "overpowered" or "underpowered" elements. This can be ensured through the concept of Game Balancing. Being one of the most important aspects of game development, it is the art of understanding all the subtle nuances in the elements of your game, experimenting with them, and adjusting them to deliver the desired experience for the player. Since no two games are exactly alike, you need to consider different factors for every type of game.

Symmetrical and Asymmetrical Games

In symmetrical games, every player starts with the same conditions. Traditional board games like *Chess*, *Checkers*, and *Monopoly* can be considered to be of this type, where it is assumed that players of roughly the same level of skill and ability are competing against each other. Balancing such games is a simple task – ensure each player knows the rules and objectives of the game and make sure they begin with the same resources (such as the same game pieces/amount of money). The focus of such games is on the strategy that each individual applies. In addition, you can have a timed aspect to the game, where each player only has a minute or two to make a move, as shown in Figure 2-4, which ensures a greater degree of fairness. There is, of course, a certain degree of asymmetry in these types of games. Questions like "Who goes first?" and "Who gets to be on which team?" can be decided by leaving it up to chance – by rolling a dice, spinning a number wheel, or even tossing a coin.

Figure 2-4. *A Game of Chess (Source: Image by macrovector on Freepik)*

Most modern-day games are asymmetrical, on the other hand. Opposing teams or players are given different abilities and resources at the beginning of the game. You might create these types of games for many different reasons such as:

- For simulating a real-world conflict or situation, where each team will have different advantages.

- For customization of the skills, look, and abilities of the characters according to individual player preference.

- To fine-tune the game according to a player's skill level, for example, easier gameplay for younger players.

- For greater replayability of the game, letting players choose different sides, characters, or items during each playthrough.

Asymmetry in games creates a bigger challenge when it comes to game balancing, but makes games more interesting and unpredictable. This is where the act of balancing gets tricky, and needs to be worked on.

Power Balance

It's essential to balance out the abilities or properties of each character, weapon, vehicle, or item to ensure that one of them doesn't significantly overpower another one in the game. This encourages the players to experiment with different combinations of resources while using clever tactics to beat an opponent or win the game. This also leads to a sense of fairness since there is no "invincible character" or "unbeatable weapon" in the game. Different characters can have abilities that counter each other, giving the characters an advantage against each other. This is very important; otherwise, it would be pointless for the players to play a game that they cannot win.

Games with multiple playable characters can be balanced by maintaining the tradeoff between the strengths and weaknesses of every character. Take the example of the game *Neopets: Petpet Adventures, The Wand of Wishing*. In this single-player action-adventure game, you can choose one of four characters (called a Petpet) to play as, namely, *Doglefox*, *Mazzew*, *Krawk*, and *Meowclops*. Each of these heroes has five attributes – Strength, Agility, Intelligence, Defense, and Health, with a certain number of initial attribution points, as shown in Figure 2-5. The higher the value assigned to each attribute, the better the Petpet is at that ability. None of these characters are perfect, since each of them has both flaws and special abilities.

	Doglefox	Mazzew	Krawk	Meowclops
Strength	6	7	6	5
Agility	6	5	6	6
Intelligence	6	5	5	8
Defense	6	5	8	6
Health	6	8	5	5

Figure 2-5. *Attributes of Petpets in Neopets: Petpet Adventures*

You can choose to play as one of the following characters:

- **Doglefox** – They are *average* at every skill, so are considered to be good enough at everything. This is what you would call the safe option to pick since all the skills are at the baseline. You can always improve a particular skill by training in the game.

- **Mazzew** – Not quite great at magic, they have *above average* strength and health but are *below average* in the other skills. This is a great choice if you prefer melee-based combat instead of magic-based, since the character will be able to deliver and receive more damage when using non-magical weapons in the game.

- **Krawk** – Having scales for protection, they have *above average* defense levels, but *below average* intelligence and health. If you want to avoid combat as much as possible in this game, you can go for this character. Since you don't need to necessarily defeat every enemy you come across in this game, Krawk is great at running away from combat without getting hit much.

- **Meowclops** – They have a knack for using magic and thus have *above average* intelligence levels; however, they have *below average* strength and health. As this game has many magical weapons, scrolls, and equipment, choosing Meowclops can give you a head start if you want to focus on improving your magic-based combat.

Risk vs. Reward

Being one of the most important pillars on which games are designed, the risk vs. reward model can determine how worthwhile and entertaining it is to play a certain game. The promise of a reward such as receiving more points or in-game money, or leveling up a character that you spend hours training can be a great incentive for players. The premise is simple – the greater the reward, the greater the risk one is willing to take, and the more investment one will make in the game. A good way to balance any game is to give smaller rewards for completing a shorter or easier task and give larger, better rewards for completing a longer or difficult one.

In games, common risks can be loss of an in-game life, the character getting crippled throughout the game (such as in the old ***Ultima*** games), loss/waste of money (made through micropayments), or facing unpassable obstacles that keep you from continuing or finishing the game. Games like ***Hades***, ***No Man's Sky***, and ***The Last of Us Part II*** that feature a

Permadeath mode spawn you at the beginning of the game if you die, making you lose all or most of the items in your inventory. Oftentimes, in this mode of gameplay, your saved file gets replaced with a fresh, new one, and you lose all of the progress you had made till that point. Overcoming this tense yet exciting, high-risk challenge can be incredibly satisfying for a player.

Challenge and Success

A common pattern or model of games involves creating game levels of increasing difficulty. The first few levels of the game are intended to ease you into it, letting you learn the basic controls and mechanics. They are usually incredibly simple and easy to beat, and players can take their time to explore all the parts of the game. Every new level introduces more game elements and tougher challenges that take more time and effort to complete.

Once the player is sufficiently comfortable with the gameplay, a lot of games start to intersperse extremely challenging levels with relatively simple ones. This ensures that a player doesn't get too bored due to the lack of a challenge, but at the same time, doesn't get too frustrated with a level that seems to be "unbeatable." An issue with this model is that the concept of difficulty is subjective; what one player deems as difficult, another might brush it off as something that just takes a little bit of effort. Then again, if a player is lucky, he or she might pass the level faster than expected.

In the game *Homescapes*, each level is classified as Normal, Hard, or Super Hard. To clear every level, you need to remove certain pieces from the game board by matching the same type of pieces together. Super Hard levels might take many, many tries to clear since they often give you lesser number of possible moves you can make and involve lots of obstacles that get in your way. Games like these usually offer special power-ups that can help you escape when you're stuck (such as tokens for extra moves or lives) in exchange for in-game money or by purchasing them through microtransactions.

Chance vs. Skill

It's nearly impossible to make a game that isn't luck or chance-based to some extent. With luck comes unpredictability, which makes games more challenging and entertaining. Many games incorporate random "loot box" systems where players get a chance to receive exclusive in-game items and cosmetic enhancements. Care needs to be taken that this system is fairly implemented, since players don't know the real chances of receiving items from these boxes or crates, and may carelessly end up splurging on them using real-world money.

The elements of randomness can either come from the game itself or from the player (since every player approaches the game differently). Take, for example, one of the simplest games ever invented – *Tic Tac Toe*. Each player gets to choose a symbol (X or O) and has to alternately place their symbol in one space in a 3-by-3 grid. The first person to get three same symbols in a row, either horizontally, vertically, or diagonally, wins. The player who goes first has nine spaces to choose from, while the second player to play only has eight. Luck plays a huge role in this game, and it is often hard to predict who will win each round. In fact, it is very easy for your opponent to get three in a row without you knowing it, if you're not paying attention, as shown in Figure 2-6. This unpredictability balances the game such that the order in which you play doesn't guarantee a win.

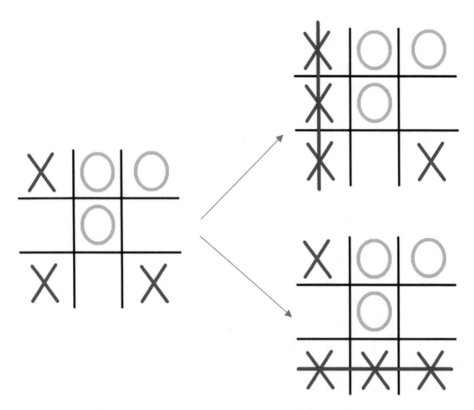

Figure 2-6. *Luck plays a huge role in winning a game of Tic-Tac-Toe*

Many games put a lot of emphasis on individual player skill, which involves fast thinking and problem-solving. Action games are often fast-paced, and rely on your ability to press buttons quickly, at the right time. In many boss fights, for example, you might have a short timing window where the vulnerable parts of the boss might be exposed. To win the fight, you need to anticipate its next move, jump/move out of the way when it attacks, and strike it accurately at the moment when you get the chance.

In the browser-based action puzzler, ***The World's Hardest Game***, your speed, timing, and dexterity plays a significantly bigger role in winning each level than plain luck. The premise of the game is simple; playing as a red square, move through the game level from one green area (the safe area) to the next, while collecting the yellow dots and avoiding the blue ones. Every time you hit a blue dot, the "death" counter increases by one, and you spawn in one of the green areas in the same level, sometimes having to restart it. The goal is to get through all the levels with a minimum number of deaths. What makes this game hard is its incredibly fast pace and the fact that it is very easy to accidentally hit one of the blue dots. Your movement and timing need to be perfect in order to pass any level.

Figure 2-7 shows one of the levels in the game. In this level, the blue dots continuously circle around the large green square where your red square starts in. You need to find the perfect time to squeeze through a narrow gap between the blue dots to reach the smaller green square at the top left. Then, you need to get your red square back to the bigger green one once again without hitting the blue dots.

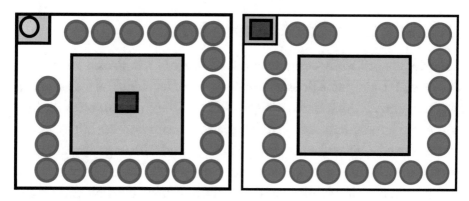

Figure 2-7. *One of the levels in The World's Hardest Game (Author's depiction)*

An Iterative Process

Since the process of game balancing is different for every type of game and is a continuous one it's unlikely that a game will be perfectly balanced for every type of player during its initial release. Due to this, many developers continue to tweak the game and release patches and bug fixes throughout the life of the game. For instance, the action role-playing game, ***Diablo III***, released an expansion pack called ***Reaper of Souls***, which added tons of new content, including a more varied bestiary and a new Adventure mode that made gameplay feel more rewarding. There was also a complete overhaul to the loot system where many improvements were made such as the guarantee that a major boss would drop a legendary item.

Teaching the Player Through Game Tutorials

A tutorial that introduces the characters, controls, and basic game mechanics is one of the most essential parts of the game. When players pick up and start playing your game, you want them to understand the idea behind it, how it works, and how to win.

Learning from Super Mario Bros.

Consider the brilliantly designed levels of *Super Mario Bros.* From its very first level, 1-1, the game does an excellent job of teaching the player how to play the game. Playing as the 8-bit Mario character, you start off at the left part of the screen, standing on a long platform, with nothing but a cloud in the sky and a hill and a bush in the background. The large amount of empty space in this opening screen gives the players some breathing room, giving them time to experiment with basic movement controls and get a feel for the game.

The area to the right is empty, which helps create affordance (the possibility of performing an action on an object or the environment), subtly nudging the player to move toward the right. This is true for almost every level, where Mario starts on the left and stays in the center part of the game screen for the rest of the level, which makes Mario's initial left-to-right movement more pronounced. Moreover, the presence of platforms encourages players to try to jump on top of them. A similar example is shown in Figure 2-8, where the floating cliffs or stones indicate that the player has to jump on top of them in order to move forward through the level.

Figure 2-8. *Open space and visible platforms in a game level encourage the player to move forward. (Source: Magic Cliffs Environment and TinyRpg Stranger Forest Pack by Ansimuz)*

Many visual cues spark your curiosity, encouraging you to interact with the game to learn its mechanics. Blocks with flashing question marks need to be hit from the bottom to reveal power-ups that can be used to turn into Super Mario (you don't lose a life when you get hit by an enemy) or Fire Mario (you get the ability to throw fireballs at the monsters) and even become invincible for a short amount of time.

Another subtle detail in the first level is in the way the game teaches you that the mushroom power-up should not be feared, and instead, should be collected. The first time the mushroom spawns after your character hits one of the question mark blocks, it falls off the floating platform, hits a green pipe on the ground, and comes toward Mario. This almost guarantees that the mushroom will collide with Mario and make him bigger, teaching you that the mushroom will help you instead of causing you any damage. You also learn that objects will not pass through the green pipes, which will block them.

At the beginning of any game, it is always a good idea to give the player some time to take a look at the surroundings, try out the character's abilities (such as jumping and shooting), and analyze the game level. If the game has a monster or enemy that can attack your character, it's best to keep that monster at such a distance that it is out of the range of the player, but is still in view, as shown in Figure 2-9. This gives the player a chance to get ready (switch weapons or armor, try shooting fireballs) to fight or escape. **Super Mario Bros.** implements this quite effectively in its first level. A small monster (Goomba) slowly makes its way toward you from the right of the screen, so you can't really keep standing in one place without losing a life. The Goomba's angry face is slightly intimidating, which provides a visual clue to the fact that this monster might be hostile, and you need to avoid it.

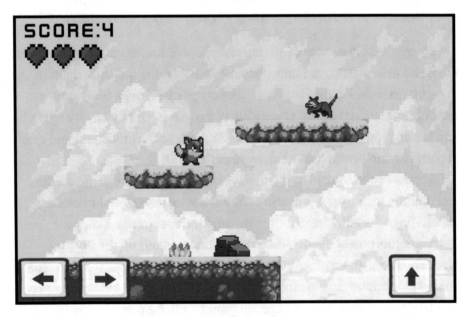

Figure 2-9. *The enemy is in view, but cannot attack the player. (Source: Designed by author using SunnyLand Asset Pack by Ansimuz)*

On the other hand, complex games are filled to the brim with tons of content that you need to learn, and the learning curve is usually quite steep. There are a lot of things you need to know at the same time in order to play the game effectively. For example, in a fantasy role-playing game like *Old School RuneScape*, you might need to learn how to catch and cook your own food. For this, the game gives you an ax, a fishing net, and a tinderbox, then teaches you how to cut down trees to gather logs, catch fish, build a fire, and then cook the fish on it. The game also introduces you to various activities such as making or buying in-game food (such as the food shown in Figure 2-10), talking to NPCs, banking, performing magic spells, mining ores, and fighting monsters. All this is done at the start of the game, on a small area of the game map called "The Tutorial Island." Only when you learn everything the game wants you to know can you enter the main game world.

Figure 2-10. *In-game food and cooking aids (Source: Ultimate Food pack by Quaternius)*

Tips for Tutorials

In many cases, giving too much information at the beginning can overwhelm the players, making them lose interest before they even reach the main parts of the game. In fact, according to George Fan, the designer and creator of the **Plants vs. Zombies** game series, a player's willingness to learn increases along with their investment in the game. This is true, since the more time you spend on something, the more likely you are to continue doing that activity with greater interest. At the 2012 Game Developer Conference (GDC), George talked about several important principles to keep in mind when designing a game tutorial:

- **Integrate or blend the tutorial into the game**

  Instead of having a distinct section that's titled *tutorial* (e.g., having an option to click "Tutorial" on the main menu), it's better and more fun for players to actively learn when they're playing the game. George says, "Teach players without them ever realizing what they're being taught."

- **Let the players learn through doing instead of reading**

  If your game has large blocks of text to read at the beginning, chances are, the players will lose interest in it. It's better to let the players experiment with the controls in a safe environment (without introducing too many game mechanics) and learn from their mistakes. This can be in the form of a simple level with the bare minimum – say a few coins, a few obstacles, and one type of enemy.

- **Stagger the introduction of the game mechanics**

  Most of the time, the player doesn't need to be
  taught every part of the game all at once. Don't
  try to stuff all the possible game elements into
  a single level or at the beginning of the game. A
  better idea is to teach the players along the way and
  introduce a few mechanics every once in a while as
  they progress in the game. This also helps to make
  the game unpredictable and exciting when new
  elements pop up.

- **Players understand a concept after trying
  something once**

  Oftentimes, if you try out a certain task in the game,
  you'll understand how to do it, and can easily do it
  without any guidance a second time. If jumping on
  top of a monster makes it disappear and makes your
  point total increase, you now know how to defeat
  that enemy.

- **Keep the flow of the game intact**

  It's not a good idea to display a message that
  requires the player to stop what they're doing in
  order to interact with it; this breaks the flow of the
  game. Instead, display passive messages that don't
  require any acknowledgment (for example, pressing
  "okay") at the bottom or sides of the screen, not in
  the center of it.

- **Use what the players already know, to your advantage**

  Games usually leverage on things that you already know, for example, the fact that spikes will hurt you, water and ice make you slip and fall, keys can unlock chests and doors, and collecting coins can increase your score and help you to buy stuff. Such elements are usually introduced in a step-by-step manner so that you can get comfortable with all the nuts and bolts of the game.

- **Use visual cues**

  They say that a picture is worth a thousand words. This is true, as images can convey messages more quickly and effectively than huge, verbose walls of text. Instead of saying "Pick up the ball from the ground", you can flash an arrow on top of the ball to make it obvious to the player that they need to interact with it. Also, if an enemy goes off-screen during combat, you can point arrows toward the direction where an attack is coming from, to alert the player.

- **Use audio cues**

  Audio cues are excellent when you want to make the player pay attention to a certain part of the game, or when you want to give the player instructions to follow. For example, the game's tutorial can have a character say to the player, "mine those rocks over there for gold and deposit the ore at the Townhall." A game can also play sounds such as alarms that alert the player to an impending battle or an attack. The combination of visual and auditory cues makes gameplay a lot more immersive and interactive.

Storytelling and the Game Narrative

Stories are an essential part of our existence – they help us understand ourselves, each other, and the world around us. In games, gameplay and storytelling often go hand-in-hand. Most game worlds are filled with protagonists, monsters/villains, companion characters, and NPCs. When players enter these game worlds, the characters they meet and encounter have the potential to make them feel real emotions, the impact of which stays long after the game is over.

Linear and Non-linear Games

Since the very beginning, a lot of games were designed in such a way that the game developer had complete control over the narrative you experienced. These games, categorized as "Linear," generally involve following a single path from the start to the finish of the game. To progress in the game, you need to go where the game guides you and complete the set of objectives it tells you to. The beginning, middle, and ending of the game are always the same, no matter how many times you play it.

Although you get to make some in-the-moment decisions such as which magic wand (such as the ones shown in Figure 2-11) or spell to use, what armor to wear, which food item to consume, and when, you usually find the items you need and meet the characters you need to interact with in the general order in which the developers intended. Because of this, every player will experience the same story and gameplay, with the only difference being the individual's specific strategy and skills used in the game.

Such games start off with a brief tutorial, after which you can jump right into playing them. You go through the game like a movie, moving around a certain area in the game and seeing the cut scenes as they occur. Think of games like ***Resident Evil 2***, ***Cuphead***, and ***Hollow Knight***.

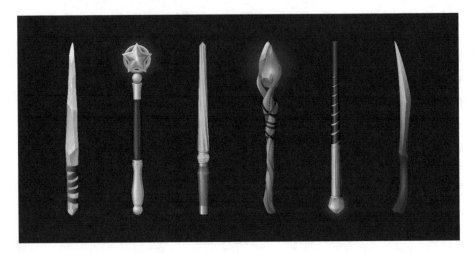

Figure 2-11. *Different types of magical wands to choose from in a game (Source: Image by upklyak on Freepik)*

This is in stark contrast to large-scale games such as Open World RPGs, which are "Non-Linear" in nature. Today, the gaming landscape is much different than it used to be. Modern-day games augment elements of linear gameplay with a greater degree of player freedom and choice. Packed with hundreds of hours of content, each playthrough can be unique and filled with previously uncovered secret paths, exotic items, and side-quests. Due to this, you can potentially play non-linear games more than once and watch as the game plays out differently.

Visiting a certain location to interact with a particular NPC first might impact your relationship with another NPC in the game. In games like ***The Outer Worlds*** where you have factions, your actions will let you gain favor with some of them while putting you on the enemy list of others! Moreover, there might also be various ways to complete a certain quest. Say the mayor of a town requires you to divert the power away from a town filled with people who have run away from the first one (again, an example from ***The Outer Worlds***). You can either fight the deserters to get this done or devise a strategy to convince them to return to the other town peacefully. Each choice will set off a domino effect of different events in the game.

Unlike linear games, there is usually no clear definition of *winning the game* in non-linear ones. The focus of these games is on giving the player the freedom to explore and make their own choices. You don't just win at the end of the game; you win every time you finish a mission, solve a puzzle, or defeat a difficult boss, all of which you get to experience in your own unique way.

Writing Our Own Stories

The stories portrayed in books, movies, TV shows, and linear games are all decided by the writer in advance. We, as the audience, can only watch as the events unfold. Non-linear games, however, allow us to live our own stories, as we get to make choices and see the consequences of our actions play out. We control the character's every move – whether it walks or runs, who it talks to, when it sleeps, when it eats. This is akin to placing a virtual version of ourselves in the game, allowing us to see through the character's eyes and live someone else's life. The plot, atmosphere, music, sound effects, and dialogue all work together to make us a part of the story, which creates a highly memorable and immersive experience.

Fun Fact   In *Detroit: Become Human*, each main character has a separate theme music that has been specifically composed for them according to their personality and behavior.

Character Motivation

Mata Haggis, an award-winning game designer, once talked about two types of motivation for game characters – External and Internal. External motivation relates to the desire to experience, explore, or change the world in a way that it impacts how others look at you and feel about you. It includes things like wanting to be rich and famous, visiting new locations, and forming and nurturing relationships. For example, in the game ***Pokémon Legends: Arceus***, you have to explore a fantasy game world, seeking out different types of Pokémon, capturing and studying them to complete a research notebook called the Pokédex.

On the other hand, internal motivation relates to the desire to change something within us, for example, by overcoming emotional issues, learning to love oneself, and becoming mentally strong. The famous indie platformer ***Celeste*** executes this concept beautifully; with dialogue such as "Just Breathe" and "You can do it," the game focuses on ideas such as overcoming anxiety and self-doubt, and trying to be a better version of yourself.

Connecting with the Characters

Games with characters can be broadly divided into two – one in which the main characters are silent, and another, in which there is voice-overs/voice-acting for character dialogues. Each of these can lead to a significantly different player experience. Titles in the first category often let you imagine the character's thoughts and feelings when interacting with the game world. This adds mystery and uncertainty to the characters, which can help a player better identify with them and even project their own personalities onto them. In choice-based games, this makes players feel a greater burden of the choices they make. Examples of silent protagonists include Link in ***The Legend of Zelda***, Gordon Freeman in ***Half-Life***, and Chell in ***Portal***.

Max and Chloe in ***Life is Strange***, Lara Croft in the ***Tomb Raider*** games, Connor the android in ***Detroit: Become Human***, and Kratos in ***God of War*** are examples of characters that have voice acting during dialogue in their respective games. The game ***Far Cry 6*** even has two fully voiced options for the main character Dani Rojas – one female and one male. Having these characters speak can make them more relatable and believable. Moreover, the things they say and the way they react when interacting with other characters gives them a unique personality, which can create a highly immersive and entertaining experience for the players.

Cut Scenes

Games are often filled with movie-like scenes, called cut scenes. These scenes play out certain key events in the game and are useful for introducing the characters and locations (see Figure 2-12), showing memory flashbacks or future visions, and for developing the storyline as a whole. They are generally interspersed between missions and levels and can help fill the gaps in the game's story.

Figure 2-12. *Castles and rocky terrain are common elements of a fantasy game (Created by the author on ArtBreeder)*

These cinematic narratives are usually non-interactive and can sometimes pop up at unexpected times. Some players may find this to be a cumbersome interruption to the gameplay, while others may see them as a good breather between bouts of intense combat or action.

Key Takeaways

In this chapter, we explored the fundamentals of fun gameplay. We learned about different types of decisions that can be made in player-choice games and saw how to create choices that are meaningful to the Player. We analyzed the concept of creating great game tutorials and learned some tips on how we can make better ones. We also discussed different ideas related to storytelling and the game narrative.

CHAPTER 3

Crafting Meaningful Experiences

In this chapter, we'll discuss different aspects of Player Progression and how leveling up, receiving perks, unlocking content, and implementing skill trees can enhance the gameplay. We'll also talk about what makes quests fun and interesting. We'll understand various movement mechanics for different kinds of games, including the concept of in-game travel.

Player Progression

Whenever you play any game, you want some way to track how far you've progressed from the start. A good Player Progression model gives you concrete signs of improvement and keeps games fresh and interesting to play. This can be achieved in a number of ways.

Leveling Up

Lying at the heart of all games, the concept of "leveling up" is core to Player progression and fits perfectly in the context of any game. It puts the focus on the growth, development, and journey of the player, packaging

© Maithili Dhule 2022
M. Dhule, *Exploring Game Mechanics*, https://doi.org/10.1007/978-1-4842-8873-3_3

it all in a way that's both visible and measurable. A level-up system forms the foundation of a game and gives players a reason to keep playing it. It makes you look forward to the next new thing and helps you use the knowledge you've learned and the tools you've obtained to try to beat the next challenge, all the while being rewarded for doing so. Seeing "Level Complete," as shown in Figure 3-1, in a game is a great feeling for any gamer.

Pokémon games have the most basic yet effective level-up system that many players enjoy – a repetitive process that involves fighting Pokémon to gain experience and level up the ones from your collection. Your Pokémon get stronger as you win battles with them, learn new moves and abilities, and even transform into amazing, evolved varieties.

Figure 3-1. *A Level Complete Screen (Source: Image by jcomp on Freepik)*

In some games, leveling up is personal to every individual, and may not always be visible in the form of XP bars, points, or level indicators. Take games like chess and checkers, for example. Every time players play such games, they use the experience gained and lessons learned from past rounds they have played to *progress* toward playing a *better* game. By applying new strategies and avoiding potential pitfalls, each player is now better equipped to beat their opponent, inherently leveling up, in a sense. Fighting games like **Dragon Ball FighterZ** and the early ones in the **Soulcalibur** franchise primarily rely on this idea. Each new fight with an opponent gives the player a chance to learn and improve their skills, which gives them an edge in predicting and countering their opponent's moves. Since this type of progression fuels a player's desire for continuous improvement, players keep coming back to such games that rely on it.

Perks and Skill Points

Sometimes, a linear leveling up system that increases the character levels by a random or predetermined amount can get predictable, and, subsequently, boring. One way to overcome its tedious aspect is by giving players the ability to allocate the points to the skills of their own choice, which puts them in charge of their own progression.

For instance, in the game **The Outer Worlds**, for every two levels that you achieve, you get to select a Perk that will enhance your gameplay. Some of these include:

- **Toughness** – Increases Base Health by 50%

- **Quick and the Dead** – The Tactical Time Dilation meter, a mechanism that helps you slow down time in the game, recharges 50% faster

- **The Negotiator** – Reduces Vendor Prices by 20%

- **Strider** – 25% faster walk speed

- **Cheetah** – 20% faster sprint speed

- **Lone Wolf** – 25% more damage when traveling alone (without a companion)

- **Deadly Demonstrations** – Receive 50% more XP when your companion kills an enemy

- **Pack Mule** – 50 kg increase in carrying capacity

- **Soliloquy** – Grants a bonus to dialog skills when you don't have a companion with you

- **Last Stand** – 30% more damage when your player has less than 25% Health

- **The Collector** – Increases the range at which all the interact-able items or objects around your player get highlighted

- **Harvester** – Restores 15% health when the player kills an enemy

- **Solo Sneaker** – Reduces the detection radius of enemies by 33% when you don't have companions with you

- **Confidence** – After the player kills an enemy, the next attack is a guaranteed Critical Hit

- **Don't Go Dyin' On Me!** – When using a healing inhaler, all of your downed companions will get revived with 25% of health

The perks are divided into three categories – Tier 1, Tier 2, and Tier 3. Each of these has 14 perks that can be chosen. Acquiring five perks from one Tier makes the next one available to you. Figure 3-2 shows an example of perks, that is, temporary or permanent powerups that can boost your skills.

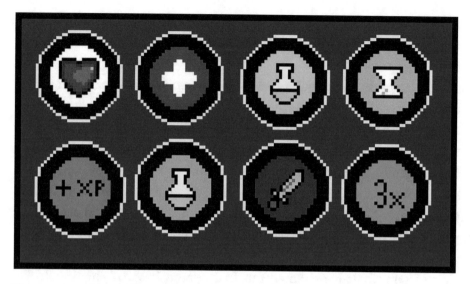

Figure 3-2. Icons for in-game Perks (Designed by the author)

Some perks even allow you to bypass certain limitations and unlock special abilities in the game. For instance, every item in the player's inventory can weigh a certain amount. Heavier armor and weapons will naturally weigh more, taking up a bigger chunk of the available weight limit. If the total weight of all your items surpasses this limit (a state called "encumbered"), you are forced to walk instead of run, and cannot "fast travel," that is, instantly travel to another place in the game. In ***The Outer Worlds***, the Perk "Traveler" gives you the ability to fast travel even when encumbered.

Unlocking New Content

Almost every game keeps certain aspects or items locked until the player reaches a specific level or performs certain activities. In RPGs, at the beginning, the player is given the most basic versions of tools, weapons, and armor, and needs to work to reach certain levels in order to wear/ use them, and to obtain upgrades and enhancements for them. Advanced armor sets grant protection for the player and can even provide bonuses to the player's stats. Figure 3-3 shows an example of different kinds of shields in an RPG game.

For example, in the game *Old School RuneScape*, you start out with a bronze sword, dagger, helm, shield, and platelegs or plateskirt, which forms the weakest melee equipment. As you level up, you get the chance to wear better, sturdier classes of equipment such as Iron, Steel, Mithril, Rune, Granite, Dragon, and 3rd Age. You can acquire these by either making them (through the Smithing skill), through monster drops, buying them from NPCs or by trading them in the game. To equip and use them, you need to have a specific level of Attack, Strength, and Defense skills (which scale up with the armor quality). In fact, 3rd age equipment, a class of items that are extremely rare in the game, has really high skill requirements and can cost billions of in-game coins!

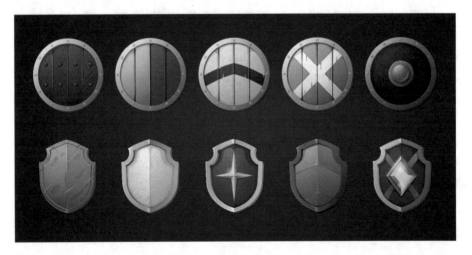

Figure 3-3. *Different shields in RPGs give various bonuses (Designed by upklyak on Freepik)*

In many games, the unlocked items don't just work as enhancements, but rather as essential tools to help you move forward in the game. One such example is *Game Dev Tycoon*, a management simulation game in which you are the founder and owner of a video game development company in the 1980s. Researching new technologies, hiring staff, and creating new games are all part of the expansion of your venture. As you progress, you unlock a variety of things such as more offices and methods of generating income. You start off as the sole employee of the company, working from your garage. Once you earn your first 1 million, you can move into a new office, which lets you hire a team of developers (after completing a management course).

Subsequent progress includes things like upgrades to your office, staff, and technology (such as better PCs and different gaming consoles, as depicted in Figure 3-4). For instance, you can unlock a Hardware Lab and an R&D lab, which gives you the ability to create MMOs and AAA Games. Your success in this game is based on various factors such as the amount of time that has passed, the amount of income you generate, the technology you have, your fan base, and the number and type of staff you have in the office.

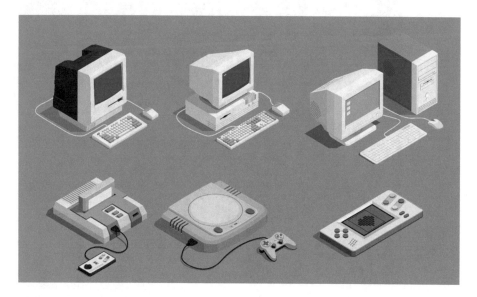

Figure 3-4. *Progression of PCs and gaming consoles (Designed by upklyak on Freepik)*

In many games like ***World of Warcraft***, you can unlock different areas in the game after you progress a certain amount or reach a specific level. Players look forward to getting a chance to explore new locations, discover and fight new beasts, and interact with new NPCs. In Figure 3-5, the character in a 2D RPG game starts out in an area with castles and waterfalls and unlocks an underground area with lava and volcanoes during the game.

Figure 3-5. *Unlocking a new area in an RPG game (Credit: Super Retro World Asset pack by Gif,* `https://twitter.com/gif_not_jif`)

Fun Fact   Lots of open-world RPG games have breathtaking worlds that are huge in size. The game *The Elder Scrolls II: Daggerfall* has one of the largest game maps in video game history – estimated to be around 161,600 kilometers large!

Skill Trees

A popular mechanic in many action-adventure roleplaying games, skill trees are a visual representation of unlockable character customization elements. They usually have multiple branches that showcase abilities that you can pick and choose from, with the abilities often being interdependent (you can only unlock a certain one after you receive the previous one in the link). This helps you plan how you want to develop your character, and ultimately, how you want to experience the gameplay.

It also gives a structure to the game and trickles out its complexities throughout the gameplay, instead of overwhelming you at its beginning by giving you all the tools at once. This is great since you will think hard when specializing in certain skills and be encouraged to use different strategies and try out various combat options, instead of just sticking to the simplest, easiest ones. Moreover, since you will be spending some kind of currency (points, tokens, score) on unlocking one of the abilities, you will inherently feel the need to use it. An example of a skill tree is shown in Figure 3-6, which involves player skills in Technology, Combat, and Magic.

Figure 3-6. *A Simple Skill Tree (Source: Designed using Image by jcomp on Freepik)*

In **Spider-Man: Miles Morals**, an action-adventure fighting game, you earn experience points (XP) from things like performing tricks while web-swinging, gathering collectibles, and doing side-quests. After you get a certain amount of XP, you receive a skill point, which can be spent on one of the abilities in the skill tree. Different branches of the tree include Combat Skills, Venom Skills, Camouflage Skills, and Challenge Skills. Each of these includes various enhancements to the combat and movement of the main character, Spider-Man. Some examples of abilities in each category include:

Combat Skills

- **Energy Syphon** – raise the Venom bar at a faster rate (a bar that gets filled up every time you attack and dodge, and once full, generates bio-electric power that can be "spent" on executing special attacks and moves)

- **Web Yank Opportunist** – yank an enemy back after sending them flying by performing certain combo attacks

- **In For a Shock** – when stunned enemies get knocked into others, they transfer their stun to them

Venom Skills

- **Venom Smash** – Smash the ground to damage and stun surrounding enemies

- **Venom Jump** – launch enemies into the air to disarm and stun them

- **Synaptic Breakdown** – causes the length of time for which enemies are stunned to get doubled

Camouflage Skills

- **Concealed Presence** – the camouflage energy bar (which gets used up when you activate it to become invisible) gets refilled 20% faster

- **Never See It Coming** – performing a certain attack called the Venom punch, when camouflaged, causes bonus damage

- **Patient Spider**– lets you stay invisible for a longer period of time

When you open up the skill tree for the first time, you can see many possible unlockables, and what each of them does, but you can only unlock them in a specific way. To be able to unlock these abilities, you need to reach a certain level or perform specific combat, traversal, and stealth challenges. With a simple and compact skill tree, it is quite possible to hit the maximum level of 30 and be able to unlock every single skill it has to offer.

In contrast, the skill trees of games like **Path of Exile** and **Elder Scrolls V: Skyrim** are incredibly massive. Due to this, there are tons of options for the player to choose from. This provides immense depth to the skills, choices, character customization, and the game storyline, but can be intimidating to even the most seasoned players. The sheer amount of content can prove to be daunting for many players, deterring them from trying out new skills.

Quests and Missions

Questing forms one of the most essential foundations of many games, without which players will quickly get bored due to the repetitive nature of the gameplay. They promise you mystery, adventure, and the greatest of satisfactions – accomplishment. When embarking on a quest, the player feels important and powerful and gets pulled into the illusion that the fate of the game world is in their hands. The chance to save a village from a terrifying dragon, travel to the farthest reaches of the world to find long-lost treasure, or try to create peace between two kingdoms that have been at war for decades is enough for players to spend hours, days, or even years playing the same game!

While the main quest makes up a huge chunk of roleplaying games, they are usually also packed with lots of side quests and missions. Gamers enjoy quests for lots of reasons, such as

- For experience points (XP) and perks

- To practice and learn new abilities such as those related to combat and magic

- To receive the quest rewards such as coins, diamonds and gems, weapons and gear, and cosmetic skins

- To unlock the next level and progress in the game

- To travel to and explore new locations

- To meet new characters and players

- To learn more about the game, its characters, and its stories and lore

- To experience challenges such as difficult boss fights

- For a sense of adventure

- For the feeling of victory, on completing the quest or mission

Quests can be broadly classified into the following types:

Gather Quests

As the name suggests, these types of quests have you running around the game world, trying to find and collect a number of things. Your character might also need to kill monsters or NPCs to gather specific items.

Some examples include:

- A cook asks you to make or find all the ingredients needed to make a particular dish

- You need to break into a heavily guarded dungeon filled with aggressive creatures to find and take a special item that's hidden within (such as an ancient spellbook)

- You need to collect a certain amount of wood, stone, ores, fish, or other basic resources needed to progress your civilization

- You're asked by an NPC to collect signatures or items or get some kind of approval from specific other NPCs

The mission "Cappy in a Haystack" in **Fallout 4's** DLC **Nuka World** is an example of a gather-type of side-quest. It equips you with special goggles and sends you on a scavenger hunt to find ten hidden Cappy mascot characters, a feat that forces you to explore and search almost every corner of the game's amusement park.

Kill Quests

These types of quests are usually straightforward, directing you to kill a certain number of creatures or NPCs. Examples include:

- Kill skeletons in a dungeon room until one of them drops a key you need to open a door

- Defeat all of the enemies on the opponent's team using your troops and units

- Kill a certain number of monsters that are a part of a task list

- Clear out an entire area filled with monsters or enemies

Delivery Quests

In these types of quests, you need to transport items or packages from one place to another or from one NPC to another. This can be in the form of:

- Delivering a message or an item to a character without losing it along the way

- A character telling you that they lost something, in which case you need to find it and bring it to them

- Obtaining the key dropped by a boss or enemy to help an NPC escape from captivity

Escort Quests

These types of quests involve safely accompanying an NPC from one area of the game world to another, for example, through an enemy-infested area.

An example is the **Age of Empires II: The Age of Kings** campaign, **An Unlikely Messiah**. This is a mission in which you need to escort Joan of Arc, a French maiden, military leader, hero, and savior, to safety. You start at a camp at *Vaucouleurs* and need to bring Joan to the *Château of Chinon*. While making this journey, you need to protect Joan at all costs, by keeping a lookout for enemy forces, and fighting them if necessary.

Interaction Quests

These types of quests involve immersing yourself in the game and interacting with its environment, characters, and NPCs. They usually require to talk to various characters, and may even involve trying to convince, lie to, or intimidate them into doing something. For example, games with factions might compel you to side with one of them and help its members fight other warring groups.

Some games don't list any specific missions or tasks for you to carry out. Instead, they leave you to explore different aspects of the gameplay and encourage you to interact with the game. An example is the game, **Twelve Minutes**, a unique, top-down interactive thriller game. It has a point-and-click adventure style, where you can click on different things around you to learn about them or use them. The entire game takes place in an apartment, with you and your wife being mysteriously stuck in a 12-minute time loop.

After every 12 minutes, a man enters the apartment, accuses your wife of murder, tries to arrest her, and attacks you if you try to resist (instantly killing you). Every time you die in the game, you turn back the time by twelve minutes, and you're back where you started. The entire premise of the game revolves around finding out the mystery behind the strange man and finding a way to break the time loop. The game doesn't explicitly explain anything to you; instead, it leaves you to your own devices to explore the nuances of the game.

Fun Fact   The game *Twelve Minutes* features over six different endings, each of which is a result of distinct choices and is a major achievement.

Designing Fun Side-Quests

When writing a captivating quest that is impactful and memorable, you need to consider a lot of factors that tie into the game. Let's take a look at some of them.

Abundance of Resources

We saw how in gather quests, an NPC usually gives your character various tasks involving the collection of different items. It is important that these resources exist in a sufficient amount in the game, and are spread out in such a way that players can easily find and access them. This also applies to kill quests – there should be enough creatures to defeat; you can't tell the character to kill 100 chickens if there are only ten in the game, especially if more of them don't spawn after being killed.

An Interesting Variety

As all quests can broadly be divided into a few set types, you want to have quests that have you do different kinds of activities in the game world. It's not a good idea to implement lots of similar quests that are just clones of each other, which can make the game feel tedious and repetitive to play. For instance, you don't want a game that is packed with only gathering or killing quests.

Length of the Quests

Depending upon several factors such as the required experience level, in-game travel, the number of resources to gather, or enemies to kill, a quest can take anywhere from a few minutes to several hours to complete. This completion time gets accumulated, and the more side-quests you have, the longer it will take to complete the entire game. Moreover, if a side-quest takes too much time to complete, players may give up on them and miss large amounts of content in the game. Any side-quest that is created should not overshadow the main quest and its storyline, else the player will eventually lose track of the main gameplay.

Balance the Rewards

After pouring hours of focused dedication into completing tasks in the game, you don't want the players to feel like it was all a waste of time. It's essential to scale the rewards according to length, difficulty, and type of side-quests. Give the players more coins or rarer, more valuable items when they undertake a particularly risky quest. For shorter, easier quests, provide the players new opportunities that they can immediately exploit at their current game level and use for advancing in the game (for example, unlock a certain skill that they weren't able to use before).

Link the Sub-quests to the Main Game

Side-quests can be quite helpful in lengthening a game's lifespan and can add value to its lore and characters. You can either have side-quests that are independent of the gameplay (in which case they act as fillers to the main content) or design them in such a way that they directly impact the main storyline.

In the game *Horizon: Zero Dawn*, you play as Aloy, a huntress venturing through a post-apocalyptic world that's overrun by machines. This game is filled with lots of side-missions that introduce you to many characters that will aid you in your journey. Your completion of these side missions impacts the allies you will acquire and recruit to fight alongside you in a final climactic battle.

Movement Mechanics

The concept of movement in games is so basic that we can overlook its importance, often taking it for granted. Whenever we play a game, we focus on what happens in the game, instead of how it happens. By pressing a few buttons we want to run, jump, and glide fluidly through the game world without any hiccups, which can make the game feel good to play. Due to these high player expectations, it is essential to work on the movement mechanics in a game, which are absolutely fundamental to the design of any type of game.

Swipes and Taps

Puzzle games that don't feature characters usually have a limited movement set. They put a lot of emphasis on how we use just a few controls to make a large impact on the game. Take for example Match-three games like Candy Crush Saga and those in the Bejeweled series, in which you need to group together the same types of elements (candies, gems, and other objects) to make them disappear from the board. On mobile devices, the only two controls that you really need to know are swiping (to exchange the position of adjacent objects, as shown in Figure 3-7) and tapping (to activate powerups). Although this makes such games very simple to play, you usually trigger a chain reaction of matches, giving you a chance to experience delightful chaos that occurs.

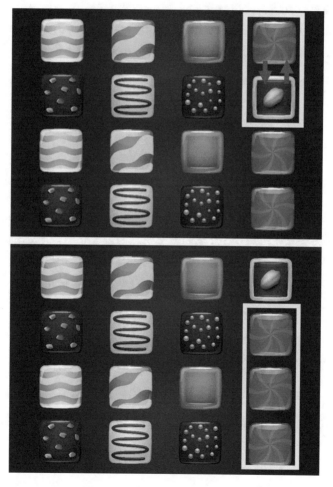

Figure 3-7. *Swapping the candies to match a 3-in-a-row match, where matched candies will disappear from the board (Source: Designed using Image by upklyak on Freepik)*

Some mobile games involve a single-tap or single-touch based mechanism. For example, in a Tower stack or Tower building game, all you need to do is tap on the screen to make one of the levels of the tower fall to the ground. The objective is to ensure that each level or block either aligns with the one below it or balances on it. Since it's a physics-based game, if a certain part of the edge of the block that's falling hits one of the corners of the previous block, it falls off and doesn't get stacked up, and you lose a life. If too many blocks fall off without getting stacked, the game is over. An example of a block stacking game is shown in Figure 3-8.

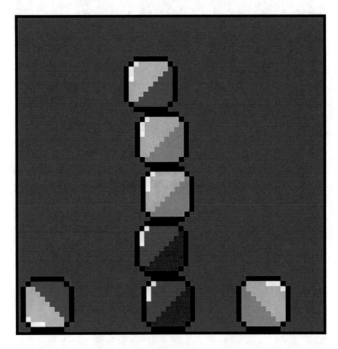

Figure 3-8. *A block stacking game with two blocks toppled over (Designed by author)*

Movement in Platformers

In many platformer games (such as the one shown in Figure 3-9), your player's movements are usually limited to a few possibilities – walking, running, jumping, and pressing certain buttons to shoot and attack enemies or to interact with other characters in the game.

***Figure 3-9.** A Forest-themed Platformer (Designed by author using assets from the Sunny Land Woods Asset Pack by Ansimuz)*

A lot of 2D games are purely tile-based systems in which the character is always centered around a certain tile, and can only move to an adjacent one (as long as there are no obstacles in the way). If you look at the sprite sheet of a certain character animation, you can see the frame-by-frame breakdown of the movement involved in it, for example, the one in shown Figure 3-10.

Figure 3-10. *Frame-by-frame breakdown of an animated character (Source: Sunny Land Woods Asset Pack by Ansimuz)*

Even with limited options, games utilize simple character movements to create new, unique moves such as dashing (after receiving a horizontal or vertical speed boost), climbing walls and ladders, flying or gliding, crouching and dodging, sliding, propelling off of walls and even double or triple jumping (jumping while already in the air). The action arcade platformer called **Vector** is one such game that lets you perform gravity-defying parkour tricks such as front and back flips, spinning in the air, and vaulting over obstacles. During each story track (level), you have to try to outrun a guard that's chasing you, while using various parkour stunts to navigate through obstacles. You only see the silhouettes of your character and the pursuer, which gives the game a distinctive, aesthetic look.

Games like ***Tony Hawk's Pro Skater***, ***Tony Hawk's Underground***, and ***Skate*** are timeless classics that let you perform amazing stunts and tricks, as shown in Figure 3-11, fearlessly navigating halfpipes and flying off of ramps. The main gameplay involves making combinations of moves while skating on different pieces of the skate park. Your speed, timing, and accuracy play a huge role in executing the perfect landing and getting a high score.

Figure 3-11. *Parkour moves (Source: Image by macrovector on Freepik)*

Isometric top-down games, such as the one shown in Figure 3-12, show you a bird's eye view of the game world. There's usually no concept of jumping in such worlds, and the character's movements are limited to walking or running around, interacting with objects like chests and doors, talking to NPCs, and fighting monsters. Famous 2D JRPGs (Japanese Role-Playing games) like the ***Dragon Quest*** games, ***Chrono Trigger***, and some titles in the ***Final Fantasy*** series are great examples. The main focus of such games is on the beautifully designed locations and environmental objects, and how the characters interact with them as well as with other characters and monsters.

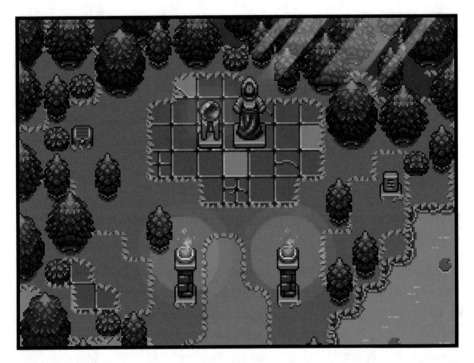

Figure 3-12. *A top-down isometric game (Source: Super Retro World Asset pack by Gif,* `https://twitter.com/gif_not_jif`*)*

3D games allow a significantly larger amount of freedom of movement for the character, vehicle, or object that you're controlling in the game (see Figure 3-13). Sunset Overdrive is a game that transforms an apocalyptical world into your parkour playground. You can make lots of iconic moves such as:

- Dashing forward while in the air

- Jumping from one building to another

- Running along walls

- Bouncing off of rooftop obstacles

- Swinging on lampposts

- Zip-lining across the city

- Grinding on rooftop ledges and railings

- Jumping to the ground from great heights

This game encourages players to cleverly use the objects in the environment to their advantage while moving at a fast speed.

Fun Fact   In the game *Sunset Overdrive*, you can move through the game world without almost ever touching the ground. You can jump on top of objects like cars, boats, shop roofs, patio umbrellas, and air vents to jump super high, and can even grind and slide on railway tracks, ropes, railings, and roller coaster tracks!

Another game, *Titanfall 2*, has fast-paced, stimulating movement mechanics. Playing from the first-person point of view, you can sprint, slide along the ground, and run against or leap away from walls. Combining these moves can make you move really fast and build exciting momentum in the game, which makes gameplay feel exhilarating.

Figure 3-13. Movement in 3D games (Source: Animated Women Pack by Quaternius)

In **Super Mario Odyssey**, a simple jump can be executed in many special ways:

- **Long jumps** cover a large horizontal space between platforms.

- **Backward** or **sideways somersaults** let you spend more vertical time in the air.

- The **triple jump** is a special type of move in which you run and then jump three times. On the third jump, your character does a front flip before landing. In **SuperMario 64**, for example, an extended triple jump even has the potential to cushion Mario against any damage when jumping off the ledge of a roof.

- The **Cappy jump** is a unique move in which you can throw Mario's cap (Cappy) in front of you when you're at the peak height of your jump, then use the Cap as a temporary platform by propelling off from it.

With lots of such moves available at your disposal, the game is all about knowing which move to use, and when. For example, chaining together Mario's jump, dive, and cap throw can result in a powerful combination that lets you jump from one skyscraper to the next. Games like *Yooka-Laylee*, *A Hat in Time*, and those in the *Spyro* franchise have similar movement mechanics that let you navigate seamlessly in a 3D world.

3D games offer the player a significant move that's hard to replicate in 2D games – the ability to zip through the air, swinging between obstacles (such as rocks, buildings, and platforms) with the help of grappling hooks. As the trajectory or arc of your swing is determined by the gravity as well as the pull of the rope, you need to focus on when to latch on and when to let go, in order to get the most out of your swing. This type of mechanic is prominent in games like *Marvel's Spider-Man* games, *Shadow of the Tomb Raider*, and *Attack on Titan*.

Action Points

Quite popular in case of turn-based strategy games (especially board games), Action Points are a game mechanic that allow your characters to perform a certain number of actions before they get exhausted. This system is prominently used in games in the Fallout series such as *Fallout 4* and *Fallout 76*. In these games, every attack move during combat costs a certain number of points, causing the Action Point (AP) bar to get depleted over time when you're attacking. Sprinting or holding your breath also consumes action points. This gives you the illusion that the character is actually making an effort, and feels tired after a certain point, which makes you feel more immersed in the game.

Traveling in the Game

Traveling in games can be a lot more fun than just walking or running. Famous examples with interesting travel features include:

- **Euro Truck Simulator 2** – In your very own truck, you get to drive along the scenic roads of countless cities in different countries like Austria, Belgium, France, Germany, Italy, Portugal, and Spain.

- **Microsoft Flight Simulator** – You have the chance to fly different kinds of planes (such as jets, airliners, and propellers), using realistic flight controls over oceans, mountains, cities, and forests that are rendered to be identical to their real-world counterparts.

- **Spyro the Dragon** – In some levels of this open-ended 3D platformer, you can fly around, destroying targets with your dragon breath.

- **Far Cry** – In games of this series, you can drive cars that you see lying around in the game world.

- **The Witcher 3** – Horse-riding is one of the best ways to get around in the game, and you can spend lots of time galloping along country roads, on snowcapped mountains, or along beaches.

- **Far Cry Primal** – You can tame and mount ferocious, fantasy creatures such as Sabretooth Tigers, Brown Bears, and Woolly Mammoths, and wade through rivers and even hunt while riding them (they will help you in the hunt!)

In some games, travel forms a major chunk of the gameplay. In exploration games, the main focus of the game is on roaming from one place to another, and observing and interacting with the environment around you. The main objective isn't to finish the game; instead, the aim is to discover different aspects of the game and enjoy the gameplay as it happens.

In a space exploration game called **Outer Wilds**, you are an alien astronaut trapped in an endless time loop on a fictitious planet. Using your very own spaceship, you can travel from one planet to another by launching into space. Since the game is physics-based, and, since the planets in its alien solar system rotate around the Sun, you need to align your spaceship with the intended planet's trajectory, and use the planets' gravity and your ship's thrusters to land on the desired location on a specific planet.

When you're very far from a planet, you can use your ship's autopilot to lock onto a certain area and accelerate toward it. Then, as soon as you come close to the atmosphere, the planet's gravity pulls you in toward its surface. Once you land, you can exit the ship to travel around the planet on foot. Since you can't breathe while standing on the surface of any planet (except your home planet), it's essential to wear the spacesuit found on your ship. Your spacesuit comes with a jet pack (that has limited fuel) that lets you fly across short distances. It also provides you with a limited amount of oxygen to breathe, which is replenished whenever you come across a tree.

The game features a 22-minute time loop that ends with the game's Sun going supernova. This means that you only get chunks of 22 minutes to explore the game world, learn about its mysteries, and find out the reason behind the time loop. At the end of every loop, you find yourself back on your home planet.

Fun Fact   The game **Outer Wilds**, which can take the average player around 16 to 20 hours to beat, has been completed by some speedrunners (players who try to complete the game as fast as they can by using determined paths and exploiting glitches) in just under eight minutes[1]!

---

[1]https://www.speedrun.com/outer_wilds

Fast Travel

Game worlds, especially those with vast, open realms, can be packed with locations that are far away due to the sheer size of the game map. Due to this, lots of games feature a fast travel option that allows you to pick a point on the map (such as the one shown in Figure 3-14) and teleport there almost instantly.

Figure 3-14. *A Fantasy Game Map (Source: Image by macrovector on Freepik)*

It usually allows you to visit specific locations that you have already discovered in the game, without having to traverse to that place in real-time. For example, in ***Red Dead Redemption 2***, you can purchase a ticket for riding on a train or a stagecoach, or fast travel from your camp to any other camp, city, or settlement you've previously been to (needs to be unlocked). *Metal Gear Solid 5: The Phantom Pain* has one of the strangest ways to fast travel – hide inside a cardboard box, and get delivered to the place you want to go!

Fast travel can be particularly useful in games for many reasons:

- You spend more time on the actual gameplay instead of wasting time traveling along the same areas repeatedly

- There might be enemies lurking around certain areas, and fast travel can help you avoid them completely

- If you forget a certain item that you need for a quest back in one area, you can fast-travel in order to get it quickly

- Some games, such as *Fallout 4*, have installable mods that ensure that fast travel doesn't consume any in-game time, and is instantaneous

- You can use warp drives to jump to a particular point in space in games with starships, such as *No Man's Sky* and *Elite Dangerous*, as shown in Figure 3-15

Figure 3-15. *Using a warp drive in space (Source: Image by pikisuperstar on Freepik)*

Key Takeaways

In this chapter, we learned ways to create a meaningful player experience, through progression systems involving leveling up, skills and perks, skill trees, and unlockable content. We also talked about creating fun and interesting quests and missions, which form the crux of many games. Finally, we discussed various types of movement mechanics involved in different types of games, also touching upon the concept of in-game travel.

CHAPTER 4

Defeat, Collect, Repeat

In this chapter, we'll focus on the process of defeating enemies and collecting rewards. We will talk about ways to create better enemies and NPCs that the player can interact with and defeat through various combat mechanics. We will also learn about how various aspects of the game economy, such as spawning and consuming resources, the in-game currency, and player inventory management, which play a major role in enhancing the overall gameplay experience.

Heading Toward Victory

In the previous chapter, we saw how quests, missions, and objectives form the backbone of meaningful gameplay. In fact, in any game, we need to clearly define the roadmap for the player by clearly establishing victory and defeat conditions. This can be done by giving players concrete goals to work toward, rewarding them for achieving milestones, and penalizing them for failing to overcome obstacles. When heading toward the end goal of the game, the player can progress in many different ways.

© Maithili Dhule 2022
M. Dhule, *Exploring Game Mechanics*, https://doi.org/10.1007/978-1-4842-8873-3_4

The Collection Mechanic

Item collection is one of the most powerful mechanics that give the player a deeper sense of engagement. In fact, almost every game gives you some sort of reward for collecting a certain number of objects, which can help you feel an increased sense of personal worth. These items can be in the form of

- Coins

- Gems

- Tokens

- Wearable and equip-able items

- New characters

- Figurines and other toys

- Decorative items

- Cosmetic skins

- Pets

Match-3 games like *Candy Crush Saga*, *Bejeweled*, *Fishdom*, *Royal Match*, and *Homescapes* are excellent examples that involve "collecting" items to win levels (see Figure 4-1). Although all these games differ greatly in the types of items to be matched (Candy, Fish, Jewels, and other icons), their graphics, storyline, and gameplay, the fundamental objective remains the same; remove similar pieces from the board by grouping them together and collect them in your inventory. Every level will tell you how many items of each type you need to collect in order to advance to the next one. If you fail to do so within a certain number of moves, you usually need to restart the entire level and may lose a life.

Figure 4-1. *A match-3 game (Source: Image by upklyak on Freepik)*

Fun Fact   The game ***Homescapes*** has a lot of time-limited events, such as "Above the Clouds," where you need to beat subsequent levels on your first try to get stacked up rewards and "Team Chest" where you work with other players to beat a certain number of levels to open up a treasure chest (and split the prizes among all). There are also special events introduced from time to time which involve things like helping a guy get ready for a big date, decorating a palace room, or solving a supernatural mystery. During such events, you need to beat levels to earn tickets, energy, dresses, or other special tokens, which you can then "spend" on various tasks, such as decorating a place.

Games like these are often packed with tons of interesting mechanics, such as

- **Limited Moves:** Harder levels give you fewer moves, and extra moves can be obtained using bonuses.

- **Time Limit:** You have to make a certain number of matches before the time runs out.

- **Explosive Matches:** Using a certain power-up can clear the entire row/column or even a large chunk of elements off of the board.

- **Super-power-ups:** Some power-ups can completely remove all the elements of a certain color or type off a board when used, while others get multiplied when activated (e.g., one power-up turns into two), having a double effect on the board.

- **Randomness:** The arrangement of items in every level is completely random, leading to thousands of possible levels of varying difficulties (**Candy Crush Saga** has more than 12,000 levels, and **Homescapes** has over 9,800!)

- **Breakable Obstacles:** Sometimes, match-able elements may be enclosed within breakable structures like stones, boxes, or walls, or even covered with things like chains, locks, bubbles, or some type of goo; the only way to remove these obstacles and make the elements inside them available for matching is by making matches next to them.

- **Creating Elements on the Board:** An example is in **Homescapes**, where a donut is a removable element that is created when matches are made near a donut creator on the board.

- **Levels within levels:** In some levels, there might be multiple boards that need to be cleared of certain elements.

Many games, especially platformers and arcade games, feature a long line of coins, gems, or tokens that your character needs to collect while defeating or avoiding enemies and obstacles. You often need to collect a certain number of them to pass the game level and go on to the next one. Different types of coins can have different values and hence contribute in varying amounts to your total score.

In the game **Rollercoaster** creator, for example, you need to draw the track of a roller coaster, so that it collects coins along its path, as shown in Figure 4-2. Not only do you need to collect most of the coins in the level to pass it, but you also need to ensure that your ride works properly, and can safely bring its passengers from one point to another.

Figure 4-2. *Author's depiction of the game Rollercoaster Creator (Source: Designed using Image by brgfx on Freepik)*

Take another example of the game **Temple Run**, where you play as an explorer, running on the stone bridges of a temple, high in the sky. Throughout your run, there are long lines of coins (the coin skins can be changed to golden leaves, cakes, ornaments, and more) that you need to collect to fill up a power meter. Once it is full, the power-up that is currently chosen gets activated. Different power-ups that spawn in the game include shields, speed boosts, and coin magnets. Using the coins you collect, you can purchase upgrades to these power-ups such as:

- **Coin Value** – Coins of double coins start after running 1500m **[250 coins]**.

- **Shield Duration** – Increase the time for which the shield is active by 25% **[250 coins]**.

- **Coin Magnet** – Increase the time for which the coin magnet is active **[1000 coins]**.

- **Boost Distance** – Certain pickups such as speed boosts spawn 10% more frequently **[2500 coins]**.

- **Score Multiplier** – Increase the score multiplier by 1 **[10,000 coins]**.

- **Save Me** – Saving the character (being able to continue the game after falling or running into an obstacle during the run) requires 1 less gem **[10,000 coins]**.

After you purchase an upgrade to a power-up, you need to spend even more coins to buy its next level. For instance, you can spend 250 coins to buy the Shield Duration upgrade, to increase the time for which your immunity to the obstacles lasts by 25%. Then, the same upgrade can be bought for 1000 coins to increase the duration by 50%, for 2500 coins to increase it by 75%, and so on.

Green gems also form an important yet rare currency in this game, and are usually scattered throughout the world. These are used for saving your player (continuing the game in case you crash or fall off a cliff) and for unlocking new characters, outfits, and gaming locations.

In fact, in many games, gems, such as the ones shown in Figure 4-3, are attractive collectibles that are perceived as rare valuables that are scattered throughout the game. Collecting these along with the coins often gives players a boost to their score, new abilities, enhanced stats, and extra lives. In the hack-and-slash type action role-playing game ***Diablo II***, for example, there are seven types of gems – Ruby, Sapphire, Topaz, Emerald, Diamond, Amethyst, and Skull, which can be used to upgrade your player's gear. These are found in different qualities, such as Chipped, Flawed, Regular, Flawless, and Perfect. The higher the quality of a gem, the better the enhancement it offers to the stats to the weapons, armor, and shields of your character.

Figure 4-3. *Diamonds, rubies, and emeralds are valuable gems in games. (Designed by the author)*

The mining game ***Motherload*** is based entirely on digging deep into the ground to mine and collect precious minerals, ores, ancient bones, and treasure found beneath an alien planet (as depicted in Figure 4-4). As you dig deeper into the ground, you find more valuable ores and artifacts, but at the same time, you keep losing fuel. If all the fuel in your tank gets used up, your miner explodes, so you need to keep returning to the surface from time to time to refuel.

Figure 4-4. *Author's depiction of the game Motherload (Designed using Image by the vectorpocket on Freepik)*

Some of the alien minerals have fictitious names like Ironium, Bronzium, Silverium, Goldium, an obvious reference to their real counterparts (Iron, Bronze, Silver, Gold). The amount of money each mineral can be sold for varies, as shown in the following table. As the depth increases, the chances of finding a rarer item increase, which serves as an incentive to keep playing the game.

Mineral/Artifact	Value
Ironium	$30
Bronzium	$60
Silverium	$100
Goldium	$250
Platinium	$750
Einsteinium	$2000
Emerald	$5000
Ruby	$20,000
Diamond	$100,000
Amazonite	$500,000
Dinosaur bones	$1000
Treasure chest	$5000
Alien mummy	$10,000
Religious symbol	$50,000

(Source: https://xgenstudios.fandom.com/wiki/Motherload)

The number of items you can collect and store at a time, the speed at which you dig, and how long you can dig depends on how advanced your equipment is; having a larger fuel tank can help you dig for a longer time before refueling, a larger cargo bay can let you store more items, a better drill can help you drill faster, and a stronger hull gives you more protection against damage. With this, the entire flow of the gameplay consists of digging underground, collecting precious items, selling them, and using the money to upgrade your equipment. The more money you earn, the better upgrades you can get, which further motivates you to try to reach the lowest depths of the game world, toward all the unknown possibilities that it offers.

Fun Fact   In *Motherload*, you can use a Matter Transmitter or a Quantum Teleporter to get instantly teleported to the surface, where you can refuel and sell your cargo. The first device costs a lot more, but transports you safely without any damage. The second one, however, brings you "somewhere" close to the surface (which may prove to be unlucky if your fuel is dangerously low)!

Popular Power-Ups

Power-ups and other pickups add a certain depth to the gameplay, greatly enhancing it. Apart from boosting your character's score and abilities, grabbing these items can even change the entire flow of the game. Let's take a look at some of the most innovative power-ups found in famous games:

- **Power Pellets/Energizers in Pac-Man:** In this classic arcade game, devouring a flashing dot in the maze gives you the temporary ability to eat the ghosts that are chasing you

- **Mushrooms in Mario games**: This well-known power-up causes *Mario* to double in size, take hits from enemies, and reach higher platforms

- **Hammers in Donkey Kong games**: Some of the games in this series feature a hammer that *Jumpman* can use to destroy obstacles and enemies (but being unable to climb ladders or jump while using it)

- **Bottled fairies in Legend of Zelda:** Fairies possess healing powers and can heal and even revive *Link* if he falls in battle

- **Jetpack in Spelunky:** The jetpack lets you fly for a few seconds in any direction, lasting indefinitely without the need for any fuel and getting recharged when your feet touch the ground

- **Morph Ball in Metroid Dread**: After unlocking, this ability lets you turn into a ball, enabling you to move faster and access areas that may be too small or cramped for you when standing

- **Time Gauntlet in TitanFall 2:** A wrist-mounted device lets you travel seamlessly between the past and the present timelines (showing a secret facility's successful past and ruined future), which is useful if you want to instantly escape enemies in one timeline and even jump onto platforms in another

Dodging Difficulties

Obstacles are essential to every game, of any type or genre. They can be physical hurdles that you need to avoid or even monsters with unique abilities that you need to defeat. When players face interesting challenges in the game, they feel more engaged, get a chance to develop their problem-solving skills, and feel a great sense of achievement. Dodging, jumping, sliding, and shooting to overcome obstacles results in a fast-paced, exciting gameplay session. Without any challenge, games can completely lose their element of fun. Let's take a look at some popular obstacles in games:

- **Rock, wood, or metal structures**

    - A prominent feature of many platformers, these structures serve as a wall that blocks players from passing through and slows them down or causes them to lose a life upon impact (e.g., trees and rocks shown in Figure 4-5)

    - May be stationary, for example, a building or a parked vehicle, or may be moving, for example, a train coming toward you

    - In many racing games, hitting or coming close to structures like walls or moving cars may do little to no damage to you, but instead causes you to slow down, giving your opponents a chance to overtake you

- **Tree branches or trunks**

    - If they're lying on the ground, you need to jump over them (else you might stumble and an enemy chasing you might catch up to you), or if they are sticking out toward the path, you can usually duck or slide under them

Figure 4-5. *Trees and rocks are commonly found obstacles in games (Source: Simple Nature Pack by Quaternius)*

- **Spikes and spiked wheels**

  - Very common in many platformers, and are in the form of either a line of pointed pin-like structures or a circular grey/silver base with spiky teeth

  - Inflict a certain amount of damage if the player comes into contact with them

  - May be visible out in the open, such as the ones shown in Figure 4-6, or may suddenly appear from under the roof, ground, or walls

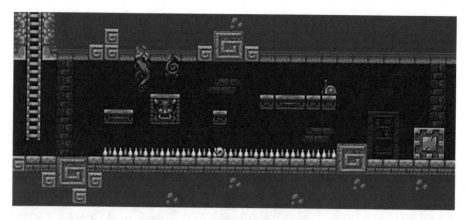

Figure 4-6. *Spikes in a platformer can cause damage upon impact. (Source: SunnyLand Asset Pack by Ansimuz)*

- **Broken paths or platforms**

  - Gaps that the player can fall through and hit other objects like other platforms or the ground, a ditch filled with spikes or water, a pit full of snakes, a large body of water, or a bottomless pit that instantly ends the game

  - Players usually receive some damage if the height between the gap and the landing platform is too much or may even lose one life

  - Bridges and platforms, such as the ones shown in Figure 4-7, may even collapse underneath your feet, which encourages you to move fast through the game level

Figure 4-7. *Bridges and rocky platforms (Source: Magic Cliffs Environment Asset Pack by Ansimuz)*

- **Fire-breathing or Steam/Laser beam-emitting statues and columns**

    - These will either periodically or continuously spout fire, steam, or laser beams at a certain length

    - Players can usually duck/slide under or run past them

    - Sometimes, you can cover the openings with an object such as by dragging and pushing a large rock or a minecart toward it, which will stop the fire or steam from coming out from it

- **Dangerous floors**

- Many games have untouchable floors made out of hot, red lava (see Figure 4-8) or those that are covered with water filled with dangerous creatures that will attack you

- The only way around them is to jump onto platforms that are jutting out, without losing your balance

Figure 4-8. *Lava-covered floors (Source: Image by upklyak on Freepik)*

Fighting Monsters

If a game only had one single enemy throughout all of its levels, it would get boring pretty quickly. This is why it is important to have various types of monsters and enemies that the players can fight in any combat-based game. Almost all major games have a **bestiary**, that is, a catalog of all the different monsters that exist and can be fought in the game. Every creature in this list is unique – each of them will have varying attributes, such as size and appearance, strengths and weak spots, and special moves.

There might be times when the player will suddenly be surrounded by hordes of such enemies (such as a large group of zombies). At other times, players have to face legendary creatures that very rarely appear in the game, but when they do, are difficult to beat and offer amazing rewards for doing so.

Combat Mechanics

Let's take a look at some of the most common tactics used to fight enemies in a game.

Jumping on Top of Them

In many early platformers, especially in *Mario* games and in *Sonic the Hedgehog* series, you could just jump on top of the enemies that are flying or walking on the ground to defeat them (see Figure 4-9). The enemy will just disappear into thin air, granting you coins or experience points for successfully defeating it. In these games, you need to be careful not to bump into the enemy from the front or back, which will usually cause you to lose a life or receive damage.

Figure 4-9. Jumping on top of enemies to defeat them (Source: Designed using the SunnyLand Asset Pack by Ansimuz)

Shooting/Slashing

Another basic combat mechanic used by most games includes shooting or slashing at enemies, while they do the same back at you, as seen in Figure 4-10. This type of combat is usually akin to a game of tug-of-war, except with health bars, instead of a rope. You need to make sure that your health bar doesn't run out before your opponent's. Food, potions, herbs, and magic can be used to replenish or even increase your total health limit and combat skills.

Figure 4-10. *Shooting at an enemy who defends itself (Source: Image by ddraw on Freepik)*

In some games, bosses have the ability to self-heal over time, and may even have a few minions by their side (see Figure 4-11) that heal them in battle. In such a situation, the player needs to first defeat the minions, before moving on to the main enemy.

Figure 4-11. *A troll enemy flanked by two of its minions (Source: Phantasy Tiny RPG Mobs Pack 1 Asset Pack by Ansimuz)*

Shooting games can also be in the form of a Space-shooter type arcade game, as shown in Figure 4-12. In this case, things like the type and strengths of your player's ship, the type and amount of ammunition, and the timing and accuracy of shots are essential.

Figure 4-12. *A Space shooter game (Source: Designed using the Spaceship Shooter Environment Asset Pack by Ansimuz)*

Using Environmental Objects

Sometimes, you can use strategically placed environmental objects placed near the enemies to your advantage. Objects like crates, barrels, and containers may contain explosive elements that you can set off and run away from, or shoot at from a distance. This will cause them to explode and inflict damage on the monsters or opponents nearby. On the downside, smart enemies can also use this against you. They can detect your exact position, and throw objects, such as rocks and barrels at you. If you don't pay attention, your character can get severely hurt during combat.

Designing Smarter Enemies

With the increased use of AI in games, enemies have become more intelligent and interactive. Let's take a look at some elements of good enemy design:

Novelty

When designing a cast of enemies in a game, there should be a certain degree of variety in their skills and abilities, and the techniques used to defeat them; the more the variation, the better. For example, in the classic *Super Mario Bros.*, you have the:

- **Goombas** (mushrooms) – move left and right, and need to be stomped on to be defeated

- **Koopa Troopas** (turtles) – they stop moving and retreat into their shell when you jump on them and can be kicked or thrown onto other enemies (if you wait too long, they come out of the shell and can cause damage)

- **Hammer Brothers** – similar to the Koopa Troopas, but they stand upright, wear helmets, can jump, and throw hammers at the player

- **Piranha Plant** – they hide in the green pipes, coming out at certain points in time, and can only be defeated by throwing fireballs at them (in later Mario games, they have enhanced abilities like spitting poison and throwing spiked balls at the player)

- **Lakitu** – an enemy that flies in the sky and throws spiny eggs that hatch into Spinies (spiked creatures that you need to throw Koopa Troopa shells or fireballs at to make them disappear), you can defeat it by jumping on top of it (which is a bit difficult since it keeps moving in the sky).

Aggro Meter

Coming close to NPCs or enemies can make them aggressive toward you for a certain period of time. If you're in their vicinity, they will start to attack you. If you run away, most enemies will try to follow you for a certain distance then go back to their initial positions. In some games, especially in many open-world RPGs, the NPCs are only aggressive toward you for a limited period of time (until their aggro or aggressive meter is active), after which, they completely ignore you. This is a mechanism that stops players from the away-from-keyboard (AFK) grinding (starting a fight with an enemy, defeating it, then automatically getting attacked by it again once it respawns) at one enemy location for hours without doing anything.

For example, in ***Old School RuneScape***, you need an attack level of 60 in order to use Dragon weapons. This skill can be trained by standing in a certain map location filled with enemies that are always aggressive to every player (irrespective of the player's level) and have high health and low defense and attack. Because of this feature, the player will automatically fight the monsters again and again as the monster keeps spawning. But after a certain period of time, the monsters stop being aggressive, and the player needs to run to a different location on the map and then come back in order to reset the enemy's aggro meter.

Announcing an Intention

When an NPC detects the player's motion and wants the player to know about this, or wants to convey its thoughts to the player, there is usually an audio cue that the game plays. This is known as a "bark," and can be in the form of a dialogue between two NPCs, or something that the NPC says out loud, for example:

- **"I thought I heard something"** – You've been detected.

- **"Who's out there? Show yourself!"** – The NPC is now alert and aware of your actions.

- **"I'm going to check over there"** – This means that the NPC is walking away, giving you the opportunity to escape.

- **"Oh, never mind"** – You're safely hidden, for now.

- **"I thought I closed this door"** – Indicates suspicion on part of the NPC, you need to be cautious.

- **"I'm hit!"** – The NPC is vulnerable, now is your chance to take action.

Fun Fact   Games like *Alien: Isolation* have extremely intelligent NPCs that can show up anywhere, adapt your playstyle and tactics, and pick up even the smallest of noises you make, making it difficult to defeat them.

Giving the Player Hints

When players first come face to face with a particular enemy, they might not know how exactly to kill or defeat it. Because of this, the enemy is usually presented in such a way that players can get hints about its behavior and abilities. This can be done by designing the enemy in a certain manner, for example, giving them wings if they can fly or putting spikes on their body to indicate that jumping on top of it is not an option for hurting them. You can also give the enemies certain kinds of weapons (according to their attack style), which gives the players an idea as to how best to defeat them. Figure 4-13, for example, shows a dragon boss. The fact that it's flying in the air indicates that you need to jump on higher platforms in order to be able to reach it to attack it.

Figure 4-13. *A dragon boss (Source: Image by upklyak on Freepik)*

It's also essential to give the players ample time to see what the enemy looks like and plan the approach for attack and defense, before jumping into the fight. This can be done by playing a short cut-scene showing the enemy and its surroundings, or an animation that shows a 360-degree view of the enemy along with its weapons, special moves, and weak spots.

Adjusting Enemy Difficulty

In any game, you don't want the player to keep fighting the same basic enemy again and again in every level; at the same time, you don't want to overwhelm the player with a boss-fight level monster, early on in the game! This can be implemented by introducing simple, low-level monsters at the beginning, for making the player comfortable with the movement and combat mechanics, and by saving the difficult enemies for later. You can first practice on the easy enemies, then, as you progress in the game, work towards learning new abilities and mastering moves and tactics that will help you win battles against more challenging monsters, such as the one shown in Figure 4-14.

Figure 4-14. *A frightening golem boss (Source: Image by upklyak on Freepik)*

Iconic Bosses in Games

Many games have given us truly incredible bosses with amazing abilities. Here's a glance at some of the most iconic ones:

- **Slave Knight Gael** in ***Dark Souls 3*** – Will charge toward you through the fog, and fight an intense, hair-raising battle with you

- **Sephiroth** in *Final Fantasy VII*– Will pose a tough fight, with special attacks such as heavy cosmic attacks, and may take multiple attempts to beat

- Bosses in *Shadow of the Colossus* – You have to fight a number of different giant, intimidating creatures, known as the Colossi, each of them having different appearances and behavior (e.g., some are found in water, some can fly)

- **Eredin** in *Witcher III* – A long boss fight that will take place in many locations such as on a ship or in an open field of ice

- **Lord Shimura** in *Ghost of Tsushima* – You get to fight the Samurai who trained you and taught you everything, truly heartbreaking

- **Ashera** in *Fire Emblem: Radiant Dawn* – You need to destroy her aura first before getting to her

- Final Bosses in *Undertale* – You will get to fight a unique, interesting boss depending on your actions in the game

- **Ganondorf** in *The Legend of Zelda: Wind Waker* – Will flood the world around you, creating torrential waterfalls, and slash at you with two long swords

- **Sephiroth** in *Final Fantasy 7* – This one has wings, and descends from the top, attacking you with special moves such as the Supernova attack

Game Economy

The efficiency of the game economy can either make or break a game. This concept refers to the flow of resources in a game, which consists of their production, consumption, and trade, and can shape the flow of the gameplay and influence the player's experience. Let's take a brief look at the various aspects of a game economy.

The Source/Tap

The source or tap refers to the point of creation or generation of resources, such as the ones shown in Figure 4-15, in a game. There can be many types of resources that can be gathered and used in a variety of different ways:

- **Wood** – by cutting down trees, it can be used for making furniture or wooden equipment and weapons (such as shields or swords), to light a fire (which can further be used to cook food or to keep the character warm), or to make building materials

- **Water** – by obtaining it from water bodies like rivers and lakes, stored in containers, then used either for drinking or supplying it to a certain establishment (e.g., a village, township or factory)

- **Seafood** – creatures like salmon, trout, shark, lobsters, and crabs can be caught by fishing in oceans, rivers, and lakes, then cooked on a fire or a furnace, and consumed to regain health

- **Meat** – by killing different animals, it can be cooked, then used to make other dishes (e.g., making a meat pizza) that can also heal HP (hitpoints)

- **Fruits, Vegetables, and grains** – by picking them from trees, farms, or vegetable patches, then using them for cooking different dishes

- **Ores** – by mining different kinds of rocks such as gold, silver, and bronze, they can be melted to create jewelry and various metals that can be used to make weapons and armor or building materials

- **Electricity** – by producing it with the help of generators, can power up equipment, buildings, or even entire settlements

- **Clothes, armor, weapons, and accessories** –can either be crafted from natural resources or bought from shops in the game

- **Misc. items** – toys, figurines, household appliances, and everyday items that can be picked up in the game or created from other gathered materials

- **In-game currency and Experience Points** – non-tangible yet essential, they are dropped by monsters that are killed, or obtained from completed quests, objectives, or other tasks in the game

Figure 4-15. *Treasure and other resources in the game (Source: Image by upklyak on Freepik)*

There might be a continuous supply of resources in a game (e.g., a steady flow of water in the river), or a timed generation where they are created in certain intervals of time. When an in-game entity is created, it is said to have "spawned" somewhere in the game. Enemies and NPCs, for example, usually spawn a few seconds after they are killed in some games, especially in open-world, larger-scaled ones. In the case of linear games or those on a smaller scale, each enemy can only be defeated once, after which it continues to lie on the ground or disappears forever.

The scarcity of a resource can directly control how valuable it is. In some games, especially those in the Mass Multiplayer Online (MMOs) genre, where the game world is filled with tons of players, resource generation needs to be carefully controlled. Since all the players will have to share and utilize the same amount of resources, gathering them becomes a difficult task in overcrowded game worlds.

For example, if a fishing spot produces a certain number of fish every few minutes and two players try to catch fish at the same time, each player will only get half of the total possible amount of fish that can be obtained from that spot. In such a case, the regeneration of depleted resources also needs to be balanced. This includes things like cut-down trees growing again, lakes and rivers getting refilled with fish, and monsters respawning after being killed. We can't have infinite resources flowing in the game either unless we want the entire game economy to crash! This is where the drain comes into the picture.

The Sink/Drain

When you have production, it needs to be balanced by consumption. The point where resources are consumed, dropped, or destroyed, is called the Sink or Drain. For example, monsters can be killed for the coins, experience points, and other valuable items they drop. In fact, the entire rate of player progression can be calculated from this process. For instance, if killing a monster gives you 50 XP points, and you need 1000 XP points to get to the next combat level, this means that you need to kill $1000/50 = 20$ monsters to advance a level. On the other hand, if you kill a higher-level monster that gives you 100 XP points instead of 50, you would only have to fight $1000/100 = 10$ monsters.

In this way, a player can advance faster and more efficiently by choosing a riskier situation, which may cause a larger drain on the player's health, items used to heal (food, potions, magic), and the time spent on the fight (it will take longer to win a fight against a stronger opponent). Both scenarios have a different drain on the enemies – 20 creatures in the first one and 10 in the second. In such cases, lower-level enemies can be spawned in higher quantities, while higher-level ones can be spawned less frequently.

Another drain in the game can be where the player spends in-game currencies like coins and tokens to buy items from NPC-owned shops or other players. Better quality and higher combat-level armor, weapons, and outfits will cost a lot more than common items that are mass-produced in the game. In this case, the shop or another player can work in both ways; as a source of these items, and as a drain that collects the items you sell to them. Other examples of a drain on resources include:

- Using basic parts for repairing broken weapons or armor

- Using up ammunition every time you shoot a bullet or fire an arrow

- Draining your player's energy, that is, action points, every time you sprint or fight

- Losing your allies or units in a battle

- Building houses, farms, and various buildings for your settlers and feeding them in a base-building game (which needs things like wood, metal, water, and food)

Killing monsters and buying/selling items are also examples of the conversion of resources in a game. When you defeat an enemy, you are essentially converting the creature or NPC into valuables that they drop. Selling these items further converts them into in-game money, which you can trade for other essentials you may need in the game.

The game economy is a cyclical structure with many interdependent entities. Every aspect of the game is linked, and changes to any one of them can have either a positive or a negative effect on the gameplay. For example, in a game, players will start out by engaging in lower-level monsters and receive smaller rewards. As players level up, they will naturally earn more coins, amass more resources, and can use them to upgrade their gear to be better equipped to fight difficult monsters and NPCs. In this way, a positive feedback loop is established. On the downside, however, you can't keep fighting the same easy monsters forever and are forced to be more proactive by exploring new areas and taking risks to try out new activities in the game for efficient progression.

Player Inventory

In most games, players can't possibly carry every single thing that is given to them or is gathered by them. Items obtained by the player are usually placed in the player's inventory. Although at first glance, this may just appear as a text-based or GUI menu, as shown in Figure 4-16, it is an essential storage element for the numerous resources collected by the player, and can be in the form of a backpack (*Pokémon*), an Attaché case (*Resident Evil*), or even a watch (pip-boy in *Fallout*). Inventories usually have an upper limit on their available space, the total weight of the items, or the number of items of each type that can be carried by the player at any given time. If your inventory is full, you often need to drop, use, sell, or store the items somewhere else (say, an NPC's inventory or an in-game bank).

Early games, such as the first *Pokémon* game, featured primitive inventory systems where players were limited to carrying only a few items that could be accessed through a menu system. Later versions of the game, such as the gold and silver versions, introduced a much more efficient and organized element called the backpack, which had several compartments, each suited for storing a different kind of item:

- **Items pocket** – to store potions, antidotes, and other items used in battle

- **Balls pocket** – to keep Poké balls, essential for catching and storing Pokémon

- **Key items pocket** – to hold quest items such as your bike, key cards, and train tickets

- **TM and HM pocket** – to store technical machines and hidden machines, used to teach Pokémon different moves

Resident Evil 4 is another game that introduced a unique inventory system. In this game, the player's weapons and their attachments, ammunition, and health items can be stored in an attaché case. Every item needs to snap perfectly in place on a certain sized grid and can be moved around or even rotated to fit the case. Players initially start out with a smaller case and can upgrade to larger ones as they progress in the game.

In many games, if the total weight of the things in your inventory exceeds the maximum possible number, the game puts certain limitations on you. For example, as we saw in the previous chapter, in **Outer Worlds**, you cannot run or fast travel when "encumbered" (overburdened by the weight of the inventory). This can work in your favor, as this mechanic pushes you to carefully evaluate every item's potential usefulness, think twice before picking up useless items, and put greater thought into character customization (such as choosing which outfits, armor, and weapons to wear or keep). It also encourages the player to deliberately use the resources they have amassed, instead of just storing them "just in case."

Some types of items such as coins, runes, potions, feathers, and seeds are stackable, hence will only take up a single inventory space when many of the same type are stored.

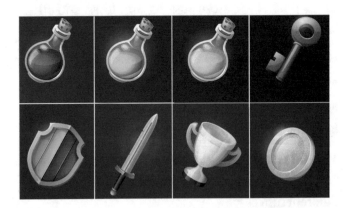

Figure 4-16. *An example of a player's inventory (Source: Designed using Image by upklyak on Freepik)*

Key Takeaways

In this chapter, we saw the importance of the collection mechanism in games, and how power-ups can enhance a player's skills and abilities, making gameplay more rewarding and exciting. We also learned about different kinds of obstacles that are present in a game, and various ways that monsters and enemies can be defeated. We learned how to design better enemies that are smarter and more interactive. Finally, we saw how the efficiency of an in-game economy can have an impact on the pace of the game, and ultimately, on player progression.

CHAPTER 5

Choose Your Mechanics

In this chapter, we'll focus on the things to take into account when choosing game mechanics, such as the game type, length and complexity, the randomness in the game, and the player investment. We will learn to design gameplay elements according to different player types based on their interest and motivation. We will also take a look at the specific, unique mechanics of a few popular games, and try to understand what makes them so appealing to play.

Mechanics as a Toolkit

Game Mechanics are a set of tools that form the foundation of engaging, exciting gameplay. The game is the finished product, filled with tons of features that impact its storyline, flow, characters, and how it is perceived by the players. That's why, for a game to be successful, it's important to pick and choose the right ones that the players will enjoy. Let's take a look at some important factors to consider:

© Maithili Dhule 2022
M. Dhule, *Exploring Game Mechanics*, https://doi.org/10.1007/978-1-4842-8873-3_5

Game Type

The game type, quite obviously, will dictate the majority of the mechanics that you choose for a particular game. As we saw previously, mobile and tablet game controls are limited to swiping and tapping on the screen or tilting the device left or right. Different variations of these include

- Steering and balancing a wooden ball on bridges, steps, and narrow paths across a large ocean, taking care not to let it fall into the water (***Extreme Balancer 3***)

- Long pressing on the screen to deploy troops at that location (***Clash of Clans***)

- Tapping at zombies on the screen to kill them (***State of Survival***)

- Swiping upwards to jump or perform stunts, and swiping downwards to slide under an obstacle (***Vector***)

- Tapping on music tiles as they appear, while following the beats of the background music (***Beatstar – Touch Your Music***)

- Steering a car down a racing track and performing drifts and stunts, as shown in Figure 5-1, by tilting the phone/tablet or tapping on the on-screen buttons to move the car left or right and to accelerate or brake (***Asphalt 9: Legends***)

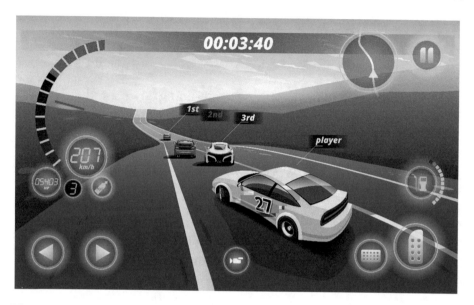

Figure 5-1. *A racing game (Source: Image by jcomp on Freepik)*

On the other hand, the control set of PC/Console based games is more vast and complex, and can include things like

- Various melee and weapon-based attacks, where pressing certain button/keys in a particular order or succession can create combo attacks

- Sprinting or dashing by holding down two buttons or keys simultaneously, for example, the one for moving forward, and the one for running/sprinting

- Gliding in the air while slowly losing altitude due to the game's gravity

- Crouching under an object such as a tree branch by holding down a button/key

- Double jumps that cause you to jump higher than normal, for example, pressing a key two times in succession

- Jumping and then grinding or zip-lining on rails and telephone lines (**Sunset Overdrive**)

- Accessing the character inventory using a shortcut button/key, and using a quick access menu to store frequently used items (**Petpet Adventures: The Wand of Wishing**)

- Using shortcuts or keyboard key bindings for consuming food, water, and potions, and for casting spells or range/magic attacks

- Clicking on resources to gather them, for example, clicking on a tree to assign a villager to cut it down to gather wood (**The Age of Empires**)

Fun Fact   The games **Legend of Zelda: Breath of the Wild**, **Immortals Fenyx Rising**, and **Genshin Impact** have similar game mechanics. Your character can engage in melee-based combat, climb buildings or mountains (with your stamina getting depleted over time) to reach vantage points from which you can spot and mark areas of interest, and fly or glide over short distances.

Figure 5-2 shows a 3D platformer game where the player needs to jump onto various leveled platforms that have monsters, obstacles, and rewards.

Figure 5-2. *A 3D platformer game (Source: Platformer Game Kit by Quaternius)*

Game Length and Complexity

Since games come in all shapes and sizes, their length and complexity can help one decide which type of mechanics to include.

Many strategy and simulation-based and base-building games take a long time to complete (are sometimes never-ending). They will often introduce you to all of the basic resources (such as an area of land, building components, and characters you can command) that are available to you, and encourage you to use them to build, create, and customize the game world. In an effort to pack lots of content in such types of games, they inadvertently present a lot of complex concepts or scenarios that may be difficult to grasp for many players. On the upside, though, if you understand how the basic gameplay works, you will have lots of interesting features to work with.

Take the example of the game, ***Kerbal Space Program***, the space-flight simulation game that lets you develop and manage your very own space program. This game gives you the chance to take your pick from over 300 rocket and spaceship construction parts, which are categorized into 15 different types (such as Pods, Fuel Tanks, Engines, and Cargo). You need to carefully choose each component according to its properties and may need to spend hours experimenting with them until you have a spaceship that can be launched into space. This may seem daunting at first but makes for a great gameplay experience for those who can get used to it. With so many basic components available, the types of rockets or spaceships you can create are virtually endless (such as the ones shown in Figure 5-3. This makes the game's mechanics excellent (though complex) when it comes to creativity.

Figure 5-3. *Different types of spaceships (Source: Image by brgfx on Freepik)*

Arcade or puzzle-type games usually have tons of short levels that players spend small bouts of time on. Lots of these become harder and harder to win at higher levels, which demotivates players to a certain extent, sometimes causing them to give up on the game entirely. If the game has good player engagement in place, it can attract the players back and give them incentives to continue playing the game from where they left off (or even from the beginning, to try to beat the high score).

Puzzle games will typically have mechanics that are simple to understand, yet difficult to master. A word-based or number-based game generally introduces its limited set of mechanics (that involve writing, forming, or searching for words or manipulating numbers), rules, and victory or defeat conditions right at the beginning, which stay constant throughout all of its levels. Take, for example, the game *2048*, with the only control mechanic being swiping/sliding tiles and merging them together. The objective of the game is quite straightforward – slide number tiles into each other to join them and get a total of 2048. You start with two tiles, as shown in Figure 5-4.

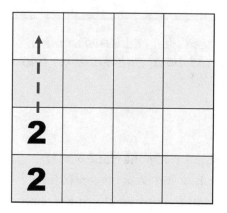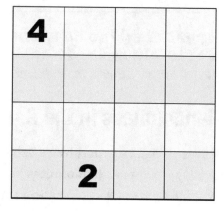

Figure 5-4. *(a) Two number two tiles being merged (b) A number four tile is created and a number two tile is generated (Author's depiction of the game 2048)*

You can slide the tiles around in the grid, and tiles with the same number will get merged and added up, as seen in Figure 5-4 (a). At the same time, a new tile with a number such as 2 (as seen in Figure 5-4 [b]) or 4 appears on the grid. Two number 2 tiles will form a single number 4 tile, two number 4 tiles will form a single number 8 tile, and so on. Each tile can end up having one of these numbers – 2, 4, 8, 16, 32, 64, 128, 256, 512, 1024, and 2048. The way to win would be to merge two 1024 tiles into a single 2048 tile, as seen in Figure 5-5 (b).

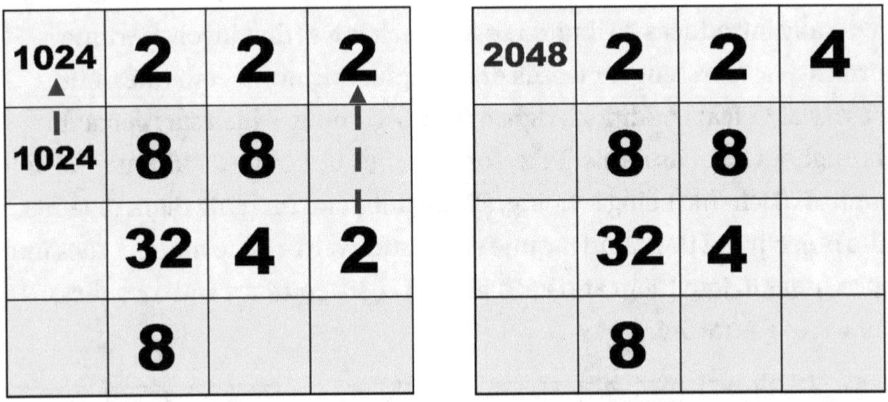

1024	2	2	2
1024	8	8	
	32	4	2
	8		

2048	2	2	4
	8	8	
	32	4	
	8		

Figure 5-5. (a) Two 1024 tiles are merged along with two number two tiles (b) A number 2048 tile is created along with a number four tile (Author's depiction of the game 2048)

Randomness in the Game

If everything in a game always behaved predictably, the game would quickly grow stale. Randomness is great when you want players to feel delightfully surprised at acquiring new items or experiencing new events in the game. For example, when you see a treasure chest, you won't know what's inside unless you open it – it might contain rare weapons and armor, potions, scrolls, food, or, if you're unlucky, nothing at all! Figure 5-6 shows an example of the different amounts of treasure that you can get when opening a chest.

Figure 5-6. *Treasure chests filled with varying amounts of treasure (Source: Image by upklyak on Freepik)*

Moreover, lots of games have monsters that drop random loot every time they are defeated. Many players will risk navigating through a dungeon, forest, or desert filled with aggressive enemies, in hopes of discovering and acquiring valuable items. Players will also kill the same type of monster multiple times for the chance to receive valuable drops, as each kill gives you a specific probability of getting a specific item.

For example, in the game ***OldSchool RuneScape***, when you fight a mini-game style boss called *Wintertodt* (a winter enemy that you need to fight by lighting braziers) and get more than 500 points, you receive supply crates (the number is based on your point total). Each supply crate can contain common items such as logs, gems, ores, herbs, seeds, and fish, or unique rewards, such as a special *Pyromancer* outfit that gives you bonuses when fighting the boss, or a rare pet bird called the *Phoenix* (*Pyromancers* are mages that can magically channel the fire from the lit brazier onto the *Wintertodt*).

The chance of getting rare items from the crates is given in the following table:

ITEM	CHANCE
Warm gloves	1/150
Bruma torch	1/150
Pyromancer Hood	1/150
Pyromancer Garb (Top)	1/150
Pyromancer Robe	1/150
Pyromancer boots	1/150
Tome of Fire (A magical book)	1/1000
Phoenix	1/5000
Dragon Axe	1/10,000

While the odds of receiving a piece of the *Pyromancer* outfit is 1/150 for each piece, those of receiving a *Tome of Fire* or the coveted pet *Phoenix* (that follows your character around in the game) are very low. The chance of receiving the strongest axe in the game, that is, the *Dragon Axe*, is even lower. Many players spend hours (sometimes soloing this multiplayer boss), in hopes of receiving the *Phoenix*. This almost out-of-reach goal is enough to keep players returning to the game. This is one of the cases in which the randomness of drops usually works in favor of the game.

At times, however, if randomness in a game is unbalanced, it can be quite annoying for a player. Sometimes, all you want to do is get from point A to point B on a map, when suddenly, a huge band of goblins come and attack you. Many classic JRPGs such as **Final Fantasy**, **Astonishia Story**, and **Dragon Quest** feature random, unavoidable encounters with enemies when traveling in the game. For example, in the time it takes you to go around a mountain, then cross a bridge when traveling from one town to another (as shown in Figure 5-7), your player might get surprise attacks by a group of monsters. This is especially true in a game like ***Astonishia Story***, where the attacks happen at fixed time intervals (every few seconds or minutes) or when you run into an enemy while walking across the game world. This may cause great frustration to the players, especially when the last thing they want to do is fight. Although the periodic encounter can be quite fun, frequent encounters will interrupt the gameplay, breaking its flow and turning players away from the game.

Figure 5-7. *Traveling from a town in the mountains to another town near a river (Source: Super Retro World Asset pack by Gif,* https:// twitter.com/gif_not_jif)

Player Investment

When it comes to any game, you want the players to feel a sense of desire to keep playing it. The more time they spend on a game, the greater will be their attachment to it. Depending on the amount of gameplay content and complexity, a game can take minutes, hours, days, weeks, or even years to complete! In games with skill-based tasks, you will naturally take more time to train and perfect your moves. The mechanics of such games may involve many complex maneuvers to execute, challenging puzzles to solve, and a focus on fast hand-eye coordination and movement.

Think of scenarios such as pushing around and stacking boxes, pulling levels, breaking walls, shooting at targets, jumping onto moving platforms, jumping a large gap between two cliffs, walking on a log kept precariously between them (as shown in Figure 5-8), or trying to get an upper edge on your opponents by anticipating their moves and using your strengths against their weaknesses. Many players enjoy these types of challenges and usually spend quite a lot of time completing them. They feel immensely rewarded upon finally opening that door, discovering an escape route, or stumbling upon a hard-to-reach elite-level treasure chest.

Figure 5-8. *A log precariously placed between two cliffs (Source: Image by upklyak on Freepik)*

Luck-based tasks fall on the other end of the spectrum and may take you many, many tries to beat until you get lucky and get the perfect conditions to win. Many games with such tasks give you the impression that all you need is skill to pass a certain level, but the RNG (random number generator) is tinkering in the background, spouting scenarios that are truly hard to beat. These games let you "win" a certain number of levels or complete specific objectives with ease, tricking you into believing that all the levels will be just as easy. The thought of "just one more try, I'll get lucky this time," makes you play game levels multiple times. To some extent, luck-based mechanics are essential, since you don't want your game to get too easy, predictable, or boring.

The game **Stardew Valley** has a very interesting "daily luck" mechanic that can affect gameplay quite significantly. Many of the activities and quests in the game require you to have a certain amount of luck in your favor for acquiring specific items. In the game, you can watch a channel called "Fortune Teller" on your television in your house, as shown in Figure 5-9.

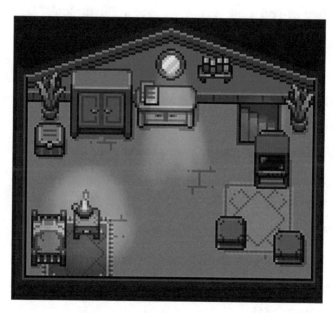

Figure 5-9. *A TV inside a home in a game (Source: Super Retro World Asset pack by Gif, https://twitter.com/gif_not_jif)*

It tells you your daily luck level (on a scale of -0.07 to 0.07), which varies every day. You'll see quirky messages such as these on the TV screen, based on your luck:

- **0.07 or better** – "The spirits are very happy today! They will do their best to shower everyone with good fortune."

- **0.0** – "This is rare. The spirits feel absolutely neutral today."

- **-0.07 or worse** – "The spirits are very displeased today. They will do their best to make your life difficult."

This daily luck will affect many aspects, such as

- The amount of coal you will get from mining rocks

- How much of your inventory you will lose if you die while mining

- Finding mystic stones, gems, crates, and treasure rooms

- Chances of receiving items that aren't trash, from garbage cans

- How much wood you get after chopping a tree

- Chances of your crops getting extra harvests

- Odds of your spouse getting jealous if you give a gift to another NPC

There can be quite a lot of luck-based aspects in the Freemium category of games as well, where the ease of passing a certain game level all depends upon your luck. These types of games make up a huge chunk of the gaming market these days. They are notorious for using strategies to pull players in for the long haul and are essentially "free-to-play," and "pay-to-win." They are designed in such a way that harder levels are quite difficult to win without purchasing and using up extra boosters, coins, or gems.

Let's take a look at some engagement tactics used by freemium games:

- Receiving rewards such as coins, power-ups, or extra lives for watching ads or logging in daily to the game (as shown in Figure 5-10)

- Getting free gifts on linking your social media profile to the game

- Being able to collect resources in the game while you're away, with an option to collect a greater number of them on purchasing premium items or features

- Waiting for lives to get refilled after you use up all the limited ones on game levels

- Ability to join a team of other members who can grant you lives

- Mixing up easy levels with super hard ones that compel you to buy in-game boosts or coins in order to pass them

- Enticing you with limited edition in-game items that you can only purchase through microtransactions

- Conducting special themed events that need to be completed in a certain amount of time, which may encourage players to play more frequently, in hopes of finishing the event before time runs out

Things like these will have players come back to the game every day in anticipation of the next unique reward. This helps keep players invested in the game for a long time since they don't want to risk losing a 7-day or 1-month "streak" after not checking in to the game one day.

Fun Fact   In the physics-based FPS **Smash Hit**, you have to throw metal balls at glass walls and crystals to break them and generate more balls. The game automatically saves your progress at a series of Checkpoints, which allow you to continue the game from there, instead of from the very beginning, in case you run out of metal balls. But Checkpoints can only be loaded if you buy the Premium version of the game!

Figure 5-10. Receiving daily rewards (Source: Image by upklyak on Freepik)

Player Types

No two games are exactly the same – each one differs vastly in terms of graphics, storyline, characters, locations, NPCs, monsters, quests and missions, and movement and combat mechanics. A game that certain players spend hours on every week might be found completely despicable by another group of players. Every individual is unique and enjoys a different type of gameplay style, content, and mechanics. While some might like flashy, time-limited, fast-paced games that rely solely on your quick reactions, others may find games with challenging puzzles that test their critical thinking skills, more to their liking. Some players are more interested in experiencing and learning about the game's lore and stories, while others don't want to be bothered with tons of text to read, and instead, prefer to jump into action-packed gaming sessions.

In order to cater to every kind of player, we need to understand what different players are looking for in a game. Richard Bartle, a famous game researcher in the MMO industry, gives us the fundamental framework of gamer psychology, known as Bartle's Taxonomy of player types. Although his theories were based on what players want out of multiplayer games, they can be applied to single-player games as well. According to the framework, gamers can be broadly categorized into four distinctive types, based on their interaction with the game world and other players: The Achiever, The Explorer, The Killer, and The Socializer. Every gamer will have a mixture of these traits, but will naturally be more inclined toward one or more of these groups. By understanding the psyche of each kind of player, we can create better mechanics that make players feel more connected to the game.

The Achiever

We are all achievers, to some extent. We play every game with the intention of passing its levels, completing missions, and collecting achievements and badges while reaching the end goal. For Achievers, it's all about the reward – in-game money, limited edition or hard-to-get gear, trophies, badges, experience points, and high scores. They are also skillers, to some extent, as they aim to max out every skill that they can, for the sake of it. Bartle calls these players diamonds (as in the card suite) since they are always looking to seek treasure. They find happiness in conquering difficult parts of the game and being rewarded for it, as shown in Figure 5-11.

Figure 5-11. *Receiving daily rewards (Image by Freepik)*

Let's take a look at some game mechanics that achievers find attractive:

Level-Up Systems

As we saw in previous chapters, leveling up is an excellent incentive for many players, and plays a key role in player progression. A gamer's level is a clear indication of his or her skills and knowledge related to the game. Advancing game or character levels can make gamers feel a great sense of accomplishment and gives them a chance to show off their achievements to other players. Skill trees, as we saw before, are examples of achievement-based unlockable systems that give players a map or a path to follow when trying to build their in-game characters with new skills and abilities. This tool gives them a clear sense of direction and guides them when progressing in the game. Achievers want to max out all their abilities and are always working toward bettering themselves in the game.

Progress Bars/Stars

When you see a visual representation of how far you've come and how far you're yet to go, it makes you feel happy about how much you've achieved and keeps you motivated in finishing a certain goal or challenge. Indicators like stars and badges give you a permanent stamp of achievement that can feel immensely rewarding. On the other hand, when you don't receive all the stars in a game level or see a "You Lose!" on the screen, as seen in Figure 5-12, it can push you to retry the game level until you get the maximum number or a "You Win!", which is the true win for many.

Figure 5-12. *Stars can be great visual indicators of progress (Source: Images by upklyak on Freepik)*

Boss Fights

What's the good in training your character's abilities if you can't test them? Monsters that are difficult to fight and defeat give players the excellent opportunity to put their skills to the test. Players also get the chance to devise a plan and use unique strategies to defeat enemies. Achievers do this by mapping out the fight arena, managing their inventory and their character's equipment, and experimenting with special moves/abilities. For instance, a player needs to acquire and store sufficient amounts of consumables like food and potions in their inventory, which they may need during the fight to heal or boost their health, strength, and abilities. They also need to equip the highest tier gear that they possess, or work toward getting this equipment from the game before they need to fight the boss.

All of this needs to be done during the gameplay leading up to the fight since once it starts, there is usually no way to escape the fight arena (unless you revert to a previous save file). Boss fights usually take place after every few levels, and serve as a checkpoint to challenge you based on how far you've progressed in the game. Moreover, these creatures are usually more menacing and complex than normal enemies, which creates a bigger hurdle to overcome and a larger milestone to reach, making the victory against them even more satisfying. Figure 5-13 shows examples of different kinds of bosses you might fight in a fantasy RPG game.

Figure 5-13. *Different kinds of bosses (Source: Phantasy Tiny RPG Mobs Pack 1 Asset Pack by Ansimuz)*

Challenging Others

Friends and other players can be a great source of competition for many gamers as they compete for the top spot on the leaderboard, inadvertently encouraging others to do so as well. Seeing your name on a game's leaderboard, as shown in Figure 5-14, acknowledges the fact that you're one of the best players in the game, which is a proud moment for many gamers.

Figure 5-14. *A Leaderboard Screen (Source: Image by pikisuperstar on Freepik)*

On a separate note, it's absolutely crucial to be careful when the game is playable online. Where leaderboards are concerned, you need to decide whether to have regional or global ones and ensure that players can maintain a certain degree of anonymity while playing. Moreover, in the case where players are able to enter text (such as while chatting in the game) to interact with other gamers, it's a good idea to use tools like profanity filters and "report abuse" buttons to filter out unwanted content.

Bonus Content

Some achievers are completionists – that is, they strive to collect every coin/star, open every hidden treasure chest, discover every hidden path, and find and collect every single collectible in a game. Including lots of such game extras can enhance gameplay and keep players busy and engaged.

Moreover, lots of major titles release purchasable expansion packs, DLCs (Downloadable content), outfits, and soundtracks. This extra content, which is sometimes cosmetic and sometimes essential for a better (or completely different) gaming experience, is actively purchased along with the base game by fans of the title. Famous examples include:

- Tons and tons of expansion packs such as **Cats & Dogs**, **City Living**, **Parenthood**, **Island Living**, and **Fitness** (each of which cost as much as the base game!) in the **Sims** Franchise

- Exclusive outfits for Alex, the main character in **Life is Strange: True Colors**

- An expansion pack called **Sunbreak** that includes new monsters, locations, characters, and abilities for the game, **Monster Hunter Rise**

- A stand-alone music soundtrack that includes all the songs of **Outer Wilds**

Fun Fact   When you play the base game of **The Outer Worlds**, the map shows you several planets, out of which four of them - *Eridanos, Hephaestus, Olympus*, and *Typhon* are locked, and you can't travel to them (unless you buy a DLC that unlocks them). So far, two DLCs have been released – *Murder on Eridanos* (which unlocked *Eridanos*) and Peril on Gorgon (which added a new planet called *Gorgon*).

The Explorer

This is a player who craves the freedom to explore new lands, visit exotic places, and meet new players and NPCs. For them, it's the journey, not the destination that counts. They work hard to uncover as many secrets of the game as possible, exploring its lore, engaging in every task and mini-game, and living through its storyline. These players focus on uncovering all the hidden features of the game, try to figure out how different aspects work, and how they can reach places that no one else has gotten to yet.

Unique Game Locations

Many games, especially those with huge open worlds feature beautiful landscapes, terrifying monsters, dangerous terrains, and random events and encounters. You can climb mountains and see lakes and rivers in the valley below, trek through long stretches of snow in a forest (Figure 5-15), or visit magnificent waterfalls.

***Figure 5-15.** A snowy forest (Created by the author on Artbreeder)*

Having varied biomes, terrains, buildings, and structures filled with different kinds of flora, fauna, and monsters can create a novelty that is greatly desired by an explorer. This can be in the form of different islands (as shown in Figure 5-16), underground areas such as dungeons with traps, and planets or multiple universes that can be visited by the player.

Figure 5-16. *An island with a waterfall (Source: Image by upklyak on Freepik)*

Most role-playing games don't reveal all of their places in the beginning. Instead, they start you out in a safe area, then encourage you to take risks to venture out to unknown destinations by giving you quests and missions in those locations. Games give you maps that have only a few locations revealed and leave the rest of them up to you to discover. Players are then tasked to find their way around in the game world, either on foot, via in-game transport, or on a mount (such as a horse or a mythical creature).

Figure 5-17, for example, shows a dungeon inside a castle that can be reached by traveling in a minecart. There is a blue portal near its center that you can enter to travel to another unknown realm. The game will push you to take this risk, either by directly indicating that you need to enter it (through flashing icons that point to it or dialogue that clearly states that you should), or it might subtly nudge you to do so (the path that you traveled on via the minecart might suddenly get blocked by rubble and debris, and there might be no other way for you to leave the area).

Figure 5-17. *A blue portal in an underground dungeon (Credit: Super Retro World Asset pack by Gif,* `https://twitter.com/gif_not_jif`*)*

The lighting, sound effects, and music play a huge role in how the player feels about a certain location. If you have a dark sky, thunder and lightning, wind blowing, and ominous music playing in the background, this can set up a gloomy, intimidating atmosphere that serves as a warning that the area you've entered is dangerous, or that something major is going to happen in the game. On the other hand, if the sun is shining brightly, the skies are clear and blue, there is greenery everywhere, and you can hear birds chirping in the distance, this can set up a lively atmosphere that's devoid of any danger.

In-Game Puzzles

Games use many props and environmental objects like boxes, stones, platforms, doors, and water bodies to create interesting puzzles that the player needs to solve in order to progress in the game. For instance, to open up a treasure chest inside the walls of a castle, you might need to find a way to open up the locked doors, as shown in Figure 5-18.

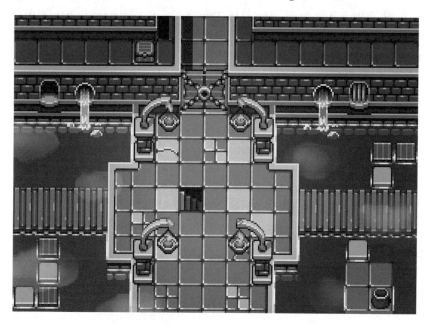

Figure 5-18. *A castle with a locked door (Credit: Super Retro World Asset pack by Gif,* https://twitter.com/gif_not_jif*)*

The keys can be found somewhere close by, but you'll first need to solve various puzzles in order to discover where it is. These puzzles use lots of interesting mechanics that include floating platforms that sink when you step on them, underground passageways, paths hiding behind walls, objects hiding at the bottom of water bodies, or fire-spitting statues.

Easter Eggs

You want to reward explorers for the thing they know how to do best, which is, of course, exploration. Sometimes, ordinary boxes, chests, or containers that hold rare weapons, armor, or items might be found in the most unlikely of places – a narrow lane behind a building, hidden behind a bush, buried partly in the sand on a beach, inside an inconspicuous cupboard, under a bed, or on top of a tall shelf that you need to climb to reach. Games usually hide exclusive items such as collectibles or player equipment in plain sight that can only be discovered by players with a keen eye. Other forms of Easter eggs include:

- Hidden messages written on paper or engraved on objects

- Cheat Codes

- Dialogues and cut-scenes that only take place if you perform a certain action

- Secret rooms or buildings

- Objects that can normally be picked up, are placed in unreachable places in the game

- Secret endings in games with multiple possible outcomes

- References to other games, books, or movies

Interaction with NPCs

Explorers want to talk to every NPC they meet, and are quite keen to interact with them. NPCs can be settlement dwellers, shopkeepers, guards, doctors, barkeepers, and inn owners, and each of them has a unique personality, if any. Modern-day games let the player go up to any NPC and talk or trade with them. This can pique the curiosity of gamers, as they try to find out the stories behind each NPC, and how they ended up where they are. By talking to them, you can also learn more about the game world as well as other characters. In fact, in most character-driven games, everything we do, such as the places we travel to and the monsters that we fight, is dictated by the people we meet.

An example of a memorable NPC is **M'aiq the Liar**, of ***The Elder Scrolls*** franchise. This humorous character essentially looks like a tiger standing upright, wearing monk robes. He is a random encounter character who tells clever, hilarious lies, and even gives commentaries about ***The Elder Scrolls*** games. Some of the things that he says in the third installation of the series called ***Morrowind*** are:

- When greeting – "Greetings! M'aiq knows many things. What is your interest? You seek knowledge. M'aiq has much. Some of it verified by actual facts!"

- Discussing the topic of Dragons– "Dragons? Oh, they're everywhere! You must fly very high to see most of them, though. The ones nearer the ground are very hard to see, being invisible."

- Talking about the topic of Multiplayer – "M'aiq does not know this word. You wish others to help you in your quest? Coward! If you must, search for the Argonian Im-Leet, or perhaps the big Nord, Rolf the Uber. They will certainly wish to join you."

- A reference to the Climbing skill, which was removed – "Climbing ropes that hang is too difficult. M'aiq prefers to climb the ones that are tied horizontally."

These NPCs are also often quest givers, and usually tell you to do something for them or acquire a certain item for them, and will promise you a reward in return. Some NPCs even agree to accompany you

throughout the game and become your companions who will fight with
you in battles and sometimes carry some of your items in their inventory.
They will follow you around in the game, and may even express their
thoughts out loud when trying to give their opinion on something. In
games with multiple companions, you can usually choose one of them to
follow you, while leaving the others at a certain location. Whatever the role
of a particular NPC, there's no doubt that they form an essential part of
character-driven games, and can be extraordinary allies or even villains!

The Socializer

This is the kind of player who enjoys meeting and talking to other players
in the game and even playing games with their friends, as shown in
Figure 5-19.

Figure 5-19. *Playing games together (Source: Image by Freepik)*

They like to listen to what people have to say, and the quality of their
whole gameplay experience depends on how others perceive them or
interact with them. Let's take a look at some mechanics that can make
games fun for The Socializer:

164

Chatting

MMORPGs and other online game types feature massive worlds filled with hundreds of thousands or even millions of people. Games like these let you customize your very own avatar and chat with other players in the game. This lets you express your thoughts and opinions freely in these virtual worlds, without the fear of being judged. Chatting is an essential social feature that can encourage the formation of in-game bonds and friendships that might last for years. What's more, many gamers find great comfort in the anonymity of the interactions in virtual worlds. Some games give you predefined options that you can choose from, such as a chatting menu filled with various phrases. On the other hand, many others allow you to freely type whatever you want to say without any restrictions (while giving players the option to filter out or report abusive content).

Learning from Others

A large-scale, mass-multiplayer game is often packed with many features that may be complex and take hours to get familiarized with. In such cases, many socializers find it useful to talk to experienced players in the game and learn about how to effectively do a certain quest or find items needed for it. This knowledge-sharing platform is invaluable and can speed up the learning process for those who are new to the game.

Trading and Gifting

A mirror to the real world, many games let you exchange items or sell them to another character in the game. This can be another player or an NPC, and generally involves bartering items, or exchanging an item for an in-game currency. Trading adds an essential social depth to games that support it, as it encourages social interaction. Moreover, it's a win for every player involved in the trade – you might desperately need an item that another person has, and you can usually buy it off from them. In addition, many casual games encourage you to invite your friends to join the game and exchange in-game lives or items with you. The games even reward you for doing so by giving you in-game money or items.

Mini-Games

Lots of bosses in multiplayer are extremely hard, if not impossible to defeat on your own. They have high health, use multiple special attacks, and usually have high defense skills. In such cases, it's foolish to try to tackle the monster alone. Instead, a better idea is to band together with a group of players and attack the beast together. Large-scale missions in games where a huge group of players attempts to take on another group of players or one or more huge enemies are called raids. This is a fun way to meet new people and play together with friends or even strangers. It's great in terms of teamwork as well, since every player will have a different gear setup, attack and defense levels, and items in their inventory. Their collective strength against their opponent can deem them victorious in battle.

The Killer

Just as the name suggests, this type of player enjoys attacking monsters, enemies, and other players. As bleak as it may sound, they find joy in the defeat of others and like to establish their dominance in the game. Let's see some mechanics that appeal to this player type:

Fast-Paced Chaos

The Killer player type feels right at home when experiencing chaotic scenes where lots of things are happening at once – buildings are collapsing, characters are falling and getting hurt, and many structures are getting completely uprooted, as shown in Figure 5-20.

Figure 5-20. *A chaotic scene (Source: Image by liuzishan on Freepik)*

Games with lots of chaos can be incredibly fast-paced and exciting. Examples include:

- **Goat Simulator** – You can run around as a goat and cause a lot of mayhem by smashing or running into everything in the game like glass tables, lamps, desks, or even people! What's more – you're completely invincible

- **Ultimate Epic Battle Simulator** – In this sandbox battle simulation game, you can sit back and watch hundreds of thousands of units fight against each other. These include Roman Centurions, Medieval soldiers, Knights, Trolls, and even chickens!

- **Just Cause franchise** – In these games, you can ride vehicles like sports cars, bikes, helicopters, speedboats, and jets, and even dive into the open sky with a wingsuit or parachute, while shooting at various buildings and enemies

- **Grand Theft Auto franchise** – One of the most popular franchises of all time, games in this series let you shoot at anything and any character, and even let you rampage through an entire city

Elements of Horror

The Killer-type players enjoy doing activities that give them an adrenaline rush. The horror genre is perfect when it comes to frightening content, and can include hordes of menacing creatures like Zombies, Ghosts, Vampires, and other terrifying monsters. These games are usually quite gory and violent and often have the first-person shooter aspect. The settings or locations have a major impact on the players and include things like mental hospitals, abandoned warehouses, or even a post-apocalyptic world. Figure 5-21 shows a scary house in the middle of a forest.

Figure 5-21. *A house in the middle of a scary forest swamp (Source: Image by upklyak on Freepik)*

Many players enjoy hacking and slashing away at monsters in dangerous locations, which gives them a great sense of thrill. Moreover, different kinds of weapons can provide various types of visual effects on the enemies, such as the stun, shock, or bleed effect. Examples of some of the scariest horror games of all time include:

- *Outlast* – An FPS set in an abandoned psychiatric hospital

- *Amnesia : The Dark Descent* – Horrifying enemies keep chasing you in the dark

- *Alien: Isolation* – An alien stalks you while you're trapped on a spaceship

- *Silent Hill franchise* – Games in this series are popular for psychological horror

- *Dead Rising* – You're trapped in a shopping mall infested with zombies, with nothing but the items nearby to help you defend yourself

- *Resident Evil 7: Biohazard* – Deemed by many as one of the scariest video games to date, this game pits you against horrifying mutated humans

Competition

Lots of games offer PvP (player vs. player) battles, which many gamers find quite appealing. Since you're fighting one-on-one with an actual person (who may be your friend or a complete stranger), it feels more real to some gamers. With NPCs, there is always a certain degree of predictability to their actions and moves. But with real players, there is no telling what their next move is going to be, which can create a thrilling gameplay experience.

Game Analysis

The secrets behind large-scale AAA games that make them incredibly famous and popular lie in the intricate and well-thought-out mechanics behind them. Let's dive a little deeper into some of these games (without any spoilers!), and try to find out just what attracts millions of gamers around the world into their virtual works.

No Man's Sky

A space exploration game that tests your survival skills in an infinite procedurally generated universe.

Type of Game

Exploration, Survival, Crafting, Combat, and Base-Building

Character Development

You begin as an alien traveler who is stranded on a fictitious planet, with a broken spaceship. You're wearing what's called an Exosuit (a spacesuit) that protects you from planetary hazards, and have a Jetpack that can help you fly in short bursts (it recharges when you're on the ground). You're given a Multi-tool, which is used to scan for and mine resources, and also works as a weapon that can fire different kinds of projectiles. An automated voice tells you to gather material such as Sodium, Oxygen, Carbon, and Ferrite dust and use them to fix your Exosuit's life support, hazard protection, as well as your spaceship, which is called Starship in the game (which it turns out, is also broken). Once you fix your Starship, you can fly upwards into space filled with a number of different planets with different types and terrains, as shown in Figure 5-22, and a single space station.

Figure 5-22. *Fantasy planets of different types and terrains (Source: Image by upklyak on Freepik)*

The Exosuit, Multi-tool, and Starship all have a limited number of slots to hold gathered resources and technology modules, which can be increased by buying them using the game's currency called units. There are various kinds and classes of Multi-tools and Starships, the lowest being C class, followed by B class, A class, and the S class (the best one). Better ones cost more units, which can be earned through scanning flora and fauna on the planets or selling resources. "Nanites" or "Nanite Clusters" are the secondary currency in the game, which can be used to buy technology upgrades.

Every space system, that is, every solar system, is owned and populated by one of three major factions or alien races – the Korvax, The Gek, and The Vy'keen. It's possible to gain or lose reputation with a faction by learning and reiterating alien words in their respective languages, giving the members gifts, or carrying out missions for them. You'll usually find some members of all three races roaming around on every space station. On these space stations, you can exchange your Starship for a better or different one, sell your resources on a galactic trade terminal, purchase maps for exploring planets from a Cartographer, and buy technology upgrades and Starships (you can own up to six at a time), and receive quests or tasks from a Mission Agent. You progress through the game by collecting resources, earning units and nanites, upgrading your equipment, exploring planets, and trying to discover the secrets of the universe while trying to reach its center. Using the resources you gather, you can craft different kinds of materials, establish a base on any planet, and build structures such as buildings and research stations.

Unique Game Mechanics

- There are over 18 quintillion procedurally generated planets having different sizes, colors, and biomes in the game, which implies that every single planet you visit will be completely new and undiscovered by other players (most likely). Every planet is of a different type – it can be calm, toxic, radioactive, extremely hot or extremely cold, and has random, procedurally generated flora and fauna (which includes land-based and water-based creatures, as well as those that can fly). Some planets are desolate, which means that there isn't a single life form on them. They usually have lots of fascinating alien elements such as floating rocks and other structures, as depicted in Figure 5-23.

Figure 5-23. *An alien landscape with floating structures (Source: Image by upklyak on Freepik)*

- Different kinds of buildings are randomly generated on the surface of every planet, and you can fly over them and land at their entrance using your Starship.

- Most planets are patrolled by robotic drones called Sentinels, which will attack you if you they detect you while you're mining. One variation of planets has aggressive sentinels that will always attack you on sight. Destroying Sentinels will continuously call in waves of reinforcement Sentinels. To escape them, you can run or travel a large distance away from them for them to stop detecting you. If you fly right into Space when Sentinels are chasing you, Sentinel Interceptors, that is ships controlled by AI, will follow your Starship and attack you. Figure 5-24 shows the depiction of a similar concept, where an alien vehicle is approaching the player.

Figure 5-24. *An alien vehicle approaching the player (Source: Image by upklyak on Freepik)*

- When traveling between planets of the same system or between a planet and a space station, you can use your Starship's pulse drive to "jump through" large distances within a few minutes or seconds. If you don't use this pulse drive when going from one point on a planet to another, you might take actual, real-life hours or days to do so, as the distance is that huge!

- There are billions of space systems, and travel between them can be done within mere minutes or seconds, by traveling through portals or jumping through space using your Starship's hyperdrive ability. To jump to another star system entirely, you can open up the galactic map, select the system of your choice, then use your hyperdrive to automatically teleport to that location. The maximum distance you can jump to depends on the capability of your hyperdrive, which can be upgraded.

- You can also jump into Black Holes or use special planetary portals, such as the one depicted in Figure 5-25, to get teleported to a completely random system in the universe. There are four colors of star systems, namely, Yellow, Red, Green, and Blue. You can only reach the Red, Green, and Blue systems when you have Cadmium drive, Emeril Drive, and Indium Drive installed on your Starship respectively, which are special hyperdrive upgrades.

Figure 5-25. *An interplanetary portal (Source: Image by pikisuperstar on Freepik)*

- There are many different types of Starship designs, such as Fighter, Hauler, Explorer, Shuttle, and Exotic, and the properties of each ship are completely randomized for every ship that lands on a space station or a planet.

Different aspects of Starships include – inventory and technology spaces, damage potential, fuel efficiency, hyperdrive range (how far the ship can jump into space while traveling to another star system), shield strength, and maneuverability.

- You can buy or acquire a large freighter (which comes with a crew) that can store all of your ships (up to six), and even send this freighter on expeditions to other star systems where it will undertake missions and collect units and resources.

- Sometimes, you will encounter pirates in space, which are basically NPC-controlled Starships. If they start attacking you, your pulse drive (which normally would let you escape) becomes temporarily disabled. The only way is to either fight them off by ship-to-ship combat or to try to move your Starship out of range and use the pulse drive when it's available again.

- One of the newest updates of the game gives you the chance to become the overseer of a planetary settlement that is inhabited by the alien NPCs of the game. Each settlement will have features such as Happiness, Maintenance Cost, Population, Productivity, and Sentinel Alert Level. By building various structures and buildings and solving disputes between the inhabitants, you can start production and raise the happiness level of the citizens. Once production starts, the settlement will produce two resources that the player can collect every 20 hours, and choose to use or sell for units.

- While on any planet, you can craft special creature pellets and feed them to the fauna. You can then adopt them as a companion (pet), and they will follow you everywhere whenever they are summoned. You need to pet them and feed them from time to time, and they will eventually grow older, at which point, they will be able to lay an egg when they are on a planet whose atmosphere supports it. You can genetically modify the eggs of companions to create stronger, larger varieties of pets, or even change their characteristics completely.

- The game is only saved every time you exit your Starship, or if you build and use a save beacon on a planet's surface.

- There are special expeditions, that is, time-limited missions where every player starts on the same planet of the same system, and have to complete a series of challenging milestones or quests.

Fun Fact   When No Man's Sky was first released in 2016, it was criticized by many as a barren game filled with meaningless exploration. Today, the game has impressively evolved into a masterpiece that consists of lots of great features such as base building on planets, the ability to adopt and ride creature companions, improved storyline and combat, planet bases that can be visited by other players, settlements, multiple game modes, and expeditions. To this day, the developers continue to release new content (in the form of game upgrades), free of cost to all of the game's existing players.

Fallout 4

Survive in and uncover the secrets of a highly radioactive, post-apocalyptic world filled with mutated creatures.

Type of Game

Survival, Action Role-Playing, FPS, Crafting, Base-building

Character Development

You play either as a woman or a man, and can customize the look and the following attributes of your character – Strength, Perception, Endurance, Charisma, Intelligence, Agility, and Luck (S.P.E.C.I.A.L skills). By assigning points to these skills, you can create different character builds, for example, one that's better at crafting, or one that is stronger in battle.

You start by seeing a pre-war flashback, a time when the world was a normal place, and you were happily living in a home with your husband or wife, your son, Shaun, and your domestic robot help, Codsworth. When the war starts, you and your family are ushered into underground vaults, and placed in cryogenic sleep chambers, as shown in Figure 5-26. At some point in time, you wake up and see your son being kidnapped, and your spouse being shot, before falling back into cryogenic sleep.

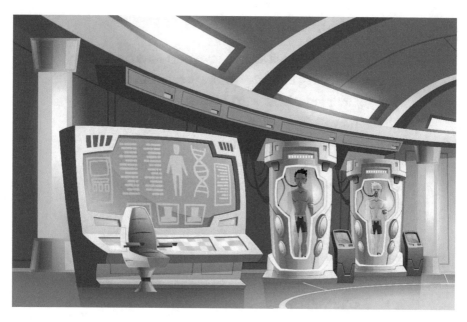

Figure 5-26. *Cryogenic sleep chambers (Source: Image by vectorpocket on Freepik)*

The next time you awaken, you're the only survivor in the vault and venture outside into the radioactive world. You're given an apt title, "The Sole Survivor." The entire gameplay after that is based on exploring different parts of the world, helping the surviving settlers, fighting mutated humans and creatures, and finding and gathering weapons, armor, food, medicine, and other miscellaneous items. The junk that you collect can be used for crafting useful items for building furniture or structures in your settlements or be broken down into basic components such as adhesive, copper, glass, oil, etc. The total weight you can carry in your inventory is limited, however, and if it exceeds the limit, you won't be able to run or fast travel and will end up walking very slowly. There are tons of interesting quests, as well as side-missions that you can undertake to discover new areas, meet new characters, and progress through the game's main storyline, which mainly revolves around finding your son.

Unique Game Mechanics

- There is unique voice acting for every character's dialogue in the game. Every time you talk to an NPC, you get four key phrases to choose from, which your character will then say, enabling the NPC to react to it. For example, when you first meet Codsworth in the post-apocalyptic world, you'll get four dialogue options:

  1) What Happened?

  2) This isn't Happening

  3) Everything is Dead

  4) You're Still Here

- Some dialogue options can only be unlocked if you have a sufficient rank of perks related to it, for instance, to persuade someone, you need enough Charisma level.

- You can collect bobby pins lying around the game world, and use them to pick a lock. Sometimes, the bobby pin breaks when lockpicking, and you need to use a new one.

- If you take something that belongs to another NPC, all of the nearby ones will attack you! However, if you sneak (by crouching) out of sight of an NPC, you can usually pickpocket the items that they are carrying, or steal items kept close to them, as long as no NPC detects you.

- There is an extensive list of Perks in Fallout 4, which act as a supplement to your S.P.E.C.I.A.L skills. Each of these skills has a list of unlockable perks or performance bonuses that you can spend your points on (which you get each time you level up).

- Every perk has up to ten unlockable ranks (some will have less) of increasing impact. For example, in the 1st rank of the Iron Fist Perk, a punching attack does 20% more damage to the opponent. Rank 4 of the same perk will do 80% more damage to the opponent, and unarmed power attacks can lead to the crippling of one of your opponent's limbs. In the case of the Locksmith Perk, Rank 1 gives you the ability to pick advanced locks in the game, while Rank 4 of the same ensures that your bobby pins never break when you use them to pick a lock.

- The Pip-boy, or Personal Information Processor, is a device worn by the player on the wrist. Along with being an information database for the player, it doubles as the inventory. You can use it to:

  - Equip armor, weapons, and accessories

  - View and fast travel to various locations on the map

  - View your stats and perks, which include your damage and resistance, health, Action points (AP), and if any of your limbs is injured

  - Keep track of your quests, and start any of them

- Keep a tab of different statistics related to your settlements, such as the number of beds it has, the population, the food and water production, as well as the overall happiness

- Tune into various radio stations or other frequencies, which play background music when playing the game

- Turn on a light that can illuminate dark areas

- There are various crafting tables scattered around the game world, including:

  - Armor workbench-to scrap, repair, or modify armor and clothing

  - Weapons workbench-to scrap or build mods for weapons

  - Power armor station-to repair or modify your Power Armor

  - Cooking station-to cook edible food and soup using animal meat

  - Chemistry station-to produce medicine and boosters

- You can wear power armor, which is a special, heavy suit that can provide enhanced protection, but needs to be charged with something called a fusion core (you need to find it in the game world or buy it from an NPC). As depicted in Figure 5-27, there are different types of power armors and enhancements that can be added to them. For example, Tesla coils can be installed on the power armor torso piece, which is capable of inflicting Energy damage to nearby attacking enemies.

Figure 5-27. *Depiction of a player wearing power armor (Source: Image by vectorpocket on Freepik)*

- The game has over 13 different companions that even include robots, mutated creatures, and a dog! Each companion can be unlocked at different points in the game and has various special attributes, perks, and interests. Whenever you choose a companion, it will follow you and support you in battle. You will also develop a personal connection to each of them as you undertake quests and missions while having them by your side.

- Doing certain actions can raise or lower a companion's "affinity" toward you, which adds additional dialogue and the possibility of romancing some of them. For example, if you choose dialogue options that are kind and respectful, some companions will like that. On the other hand, lying and stealing are strongly disliked by some of them, and will cause their affinity towards you to decrease.

- Your companions can carry items for you, and you can also equip them with gear, weapons, and accessories.

- Fallout 4 features a Vault-Tec Assisted Targeting System (V.A.T.S.), which can be used in combat to slow down time and target various areas of the enemy when attacking it.

- There are tons of different kinds of weapons in the game, ranging from pistols, rifles, machine guns, baseball bats, and even nuclear ones.

- The player can sleep on beds or sleeping bags, or sit on chairs, stools, or couches to pass time.

Fun Fact   In *Fallout 4*, you can add Mods or modifications that can enhance or even completely change the gameplay. There are mods for all kinds of things – the ability to carry infinite weight, to have two companions with you at the same time, to have infinite ammo, AP, and health, invincibility mods (your character suffers absolutely no damage in combat), mods that let you create NPCs and items for your settlement, and even those that add new quests and entirely new storylines to the game!

Life Is Strange

Play as an ordinary high school teenager who has the ability to rewind time, affecting the past, present, and future.

Type of Game

Graphic Adventure, Player Choice

Character Development

You play as Max Caulfield, an aspiring photographer who returns to her hometown, Arcadia Bay, Oregon, the place where she grew up. After seeing Chloe Price, her childhood friend, being killed, Max discovers that she now has the ability to rewind time, and goes back in time to save her. Max is a character who likes to observe the world around her and capture her surroundings in her photographs, as shown in Figure 5-28. She reconnects with Chloe, her classmates, as well as the residents of her town, learning more about them. During this time, there is a threat of a looming storm that is heading toward the town. Max sees a future vision of the town being hit by a giant tornado, destroying everything in its path. Throughout the entire game, she's trying to figure out a way to stop the impending threat and save her beloved town and its residents.

Figure 5-28. *Taking a photo to capture the moment (Source: Image by storyset on Freepik)*

Unique Game Mechanics

- You play the game in a series of episodes, and you can only go on to the next one after completing the current one.

- This is a story-based game where every player choice will show you a different cut-scene and NPC reactions. All the decisions you make affect the past, present, and future of the game, and directly dictate how the future will play out and the storyline you will experience.

- In every episode, you are confined to a certain game location where you need to walk around and interact with the characters and the world around you. If you see something happening that you feel could have been avoided, you can reverse time and perform a different action to get a new outcome. For example, if you see a friend getting hit by a ball, you can rewind time and warn him or her to get out of the way before the ball gets thrown in their direction.

- In the game world, you can take photos of certain special items, people, animals, other photos, etc. These photos act as collectibles and add to your achievement list.

- At the end of every episode, you get to see all the choices you made in the game, and also see how many percent of other players made which choice. You can always go back to a certain chapter in an episode, and replay the game with different choices.

- The game has multiple emotionally driven storylines that deliver powerful messages around how an individual's choices affect the world around them. It also focuses on many real-world issues that players feel connected to, and, through player choice, encourages players to take responsibility for their actions.

- There are no specific victory conditions in the game, as the focus is on experiencing the game as it unfolds.

Fun Fact   There are three major titles in the ***Life is Strange*** Franchise, in which the main characters have different supernatural powers. In the first game, Max Caulfield has the ability to rewind time. In ***Life is Strange 2***, Daniel Diaz has the power of telekinesis – which lets him move and throw objects with his mind. In the third installment of the series, ***Life is Strange: True Colors***, Alex holds a psychic power that lets her see people's emotional states in the form of colorful auras around them.

Key Takeaways

In this chapter, we talked about how game mechanics are a set of tools that we can use for creating a meaningful gameplay experience. We discussed factors that we need to consider while choosing mechanics for different kinds of games and players. We learned about the four major types of gaming personalities, and the various mechanics that each of them prefers. Finally, we took a look at the specific mechanics involved in a few popular games.

Index

A

Achievers
    bonus content, 156, 157
    boss flights, 154, 155
    challenging, 155, 156
    level-up systems, 152
    progress bars/stars, 153
Action-adventure games,
    21–28, 46, 50
Adventure mode, 56
Alien landscape, 173
Alien vehicle, 173, 174
Award-winning franchise, 18
Award-winning game
    designer, 65
Away-from-keyboard (AFK), 121

B

Balancing, 24, 37, 47–49, 55, 136
Balls pocket, 131
Base-building games, 15–17, 139
Breakable obstacles, 104
Browser-based action
    puzzler, 54
Butterfly effect, 45

C

Candy Crush, 13, 14, 86,
    102, 104
Cappy jump, 95
Chance *vs.* Skill, 53–55
Choice-based games, 42, 46, 66
Cinematic narratives, 68
Combat mechanics
    environmental objects, 119
    jumping on top, 116
    shooting/slashing, 117–119
Cut scenes, 27, 63, 67–68, 162
Cut the Rope series, 12–13

D

Dodging
    broken paths/platforms,
      113, 114
    dangerous floors, 114
    fire-breathing/steam/laser
      beam, 114
    rock/wood/metal
      structures, 111
    spikes/spiked wheels, 112
    tree branches/trunks, 111

© Maithili Dhule 2022
M. Dhule, *Exploring Game Mechanics*, https://doi.org/10.1007/978-1-4842-8873-3

Printed in the United States
by Baker & Taylor Publisher Services